BRANDING
EDGE

Elevating Excellence
Through Hedge Fund Identity

NATASHA B. KOPRIVICA

"The best way to predict the future is to create it."
— Peter Drucker, *Pioneer of Modern Business Strategy*

Introduction

I n the hedge fund industry, performance is often described as the ultimate brand. Numbers, after all, speak loudly. But experience has shown me that numbers alone rarely secure enduring capital. Allocators do not merely underwrite a return stream; they underwrite conviction, philosophy, and trust. They invest in the story behind the numbers, and in the people who can consistently deliver that story with clarity and integrity.

Branding, therefore, is not a surface exercise. It is not the logo on your deck, the tagline on your website, or the polish of your investor letter. True branding is the alignment of identity, purpose, and presence. It is the way your fund demonstrates, day after day, that it understands what allocators are trying to solve, that it occupies a distinct place in the market, and that it stands for something beyond quarterly returns.

Over the past twenty-five years, I have sat across the table from endowments, family offices, pensions, and sovereign funds on three continents. I have seen promising managers fail to raise capital despite strong performance, and I have seen others attract enduring loyalty through something more powerful: authenticity. The funds that succeed long term do not try to be louder than the competition, they strive to be clearer. Their values and strategy are so deeply lived that their brand cannot be separated from who they are.

This principle echoes an ancient truth. The Indian mystic and spiritual teacher Sadhguru, widely known for his insights on human consciousness and leadership, often speaks about identity as both a source of strength and a potential limitation. He warns that clinging to borrowed or superficial identities makes us rigid, while authentic alignment of who we are and what we do creates clarity and vitality. In his words, "If you are intense enough in your experience, the world cannot ignore you." Applied to the investment world, this means that branding is not about performance theater or self-promotion. It is about cultivating a depth of conviction so real that allocators recognize it instinctively.

This book is written with a wide audience in mind: hedge fund managers launching or scaling their firms, executives shaping organizational identity, marketing and sales professionals seeking more effective engagement with allocators, and students preparing to enter the industry. It will not offer shortcuts. Instead, it will challenge you to reframe branding as a strategic advantage, as critical to raising and retaining capital as risk management or portfolio construction. You will see how great funds, from global titans to niche boutiques, built brands that outlived market cycles and became magnets for capital.

In preparing this work, I drew on extensive research, conversations with branding experts, allocator perspectives, and the lessons of lived experience. I consulted books written by branding, business, and storytelling experts in this task and have spoken to investors of different preferences and backgrounds with professional writers; my purpose is simply to shed light on a subject and make it clearer for many in the industry. Alongside these, I made use of modern writing tools such as ChatGPT and QuillBot for research, structure to support the process. My intent is not to showcase my writing skills or compete

Most importantly, I am grateful to everyone who worked with me, shared their perspectives, and inspired me to bring this project to completion.

My hope is that the pages ahead will inspire you to approach branding not as an afterthought, but as a core discipline, one that elevates your fund from being yet another name in a database to becoming a trusted, enduring partner in an allocator's portfolio.

Natasha B. Koprivica

Dedication

To my husband, Michael, whose unwavering support and belief sustain me in all that I do. Your presence brings balance to every challenge and meaning to every success.

To Aleksandar and Teodor, may your curiosity and courage always lead you to explore what is possible and achieve what you imagine. May you always know that my greatest pride is watching you grow into the best versions of yourselves.

To my family in Serbia and the United States, whose support and understanding have grounded me through every season of life. Your love reminds me that every achievement begins with belonging.

Perspectives from Industry Leaders

"Natasha Koprivica has written the book the hedge fund industry didn't know it needed. Her perspective on brand equity is unparalleled. Branding Edge challenges the status quo, reminding us that while numbers open doors, it is the clarity of narrative and integrity of identity that secure long-term trust. For those seeking to differentiate themselves in a crowded marketplace, this is the blueprint for success."

Jinhee Suh
Chief Investment Officer
Global Investments NH-Amundi Asset Management

"Branding Edge captures a hard truth in asset management: performance is essential, but not sufficient. Through clear, practical frameworks, it shows how clarity, conviction, and disciplined positioning are what ultimately earn institutional trust."

Masayuki Abe,
Chief Product Manager,
Mitsubishi UFJ Trust and Banking Corporation

"Branding Edge is a powerful reminder that purpose and trust are the real differentiators in asset management. It challenges managers to define the 'why' behind their work and to communicate it with clarity and conviction. For leaders committed to building investment platforms that stand for something, this book is indispensable."

Havell Rodrigues, CAIA
CEO & Managing Partner,
New Majority Capital, LLC

"In Branding Edge, Natasha Koprivica challenges the hedge fund industry to rethink how it communicates with investors. By integrating investor psychology with a disciplined brand framework, she shows how complex strategies and digital narratives can be delivered with greater clarity, relevance, and lasting impact in an increasingly competitive capital-raising environment."

Brandy Whelan
Vice President of Channel Marketing
Formerly, Fidelity Investments

"Across real-world examples, historical context, and allocator perspectives, this book explains why so many managers sound the same, and what the most successful firms do differently in how they position, communicate, and live their strategy every day. You will see how branding evolved from a late afterthought in asset management into a strategic discipline shaped by digital media, increased due diligence, and shifting investor expectations."

In Branding Edge, Natasha Koprivica articulates what many in asset management have sensed yet rarely expressed clearly: branding is coherence made visible. When a manager's strategy, behavior, culture, and communication are truly aligned, allocators instinctively feel it. Trust is built not only through performance but also through structural integrity over time. This book elevates branding from surface positioning to disciplined alignment, offering managers a powerful path toward authenticity, clarity, and enduring institutional trust."

Appendix

Appendix A

A structured set of diagnostic questions covering identity, strategy, positioning, and communication.

Appendix B

Detailed profiles of allocator types, including priorities, constraints, and decision criteria.

Appendix C

Thirty positioning approaches demonstrating different ways to define and communicate differentiation.

Appendix D

A complete framework for strategy, messaging, visual identity, voice, and governance to ensure consistency.

Table of Contents

CHAPTER ONE

Why Branding Became Necessary

"Endurance is one of the most difficult disciplines, but it is to the one who endures that the final victory comes."

Buddha, Dhammapada, 3rd century BCE

A Perfect Storm

The last decade witnessed the longest bull market in recorded history (Schroders, 2018). Between March 9, 2009, and August 22, 2018, the world experienced one of the longest bull markets in history. It lasted nine years, five months, and thirteen days. "The S&P 500 has had more than 50 new highs in 2021 alone" (Young, 2022).

It was mid-morning, but it already felt like a full day had passed. The scent of fresh coffee mingled with the low hum of market alerts streaming from Bloomberg TV in the background. We had just moved from Boston to our house in Providence, boxes still half packed,

WiFi barely functional, and my makeshift workstation set up in the corner of the living room. I stood watching the screen, coffee cooling in my hand, as the breaking news rolled in. A global pandemic. Market turmoil accelerating by the minute. Volatility indexes spiking. Headlines stacking one on top of the other like a series of aftershocks. The world was holding its breath.

And I remember thinking, "Here we go again." I had seen this movie before. Crisis. Fear. Flight to safety. "This kind of volatility is rare, a moment for the hedge funds to step up. Let us hope."

In recent years, actively managed strategies have struggled to attract capital, as investors pulled back due to underperformance relative to the broader market and the burden of high fees. According to the eVestment report (2021), actively managed hedge funds saw a total outflow of 194.1 billion dollars over the past three years.

While most investors recognize that the bull market will not last forever and that prudent hedging is essential, overall market confidence remains high at the time of writing. Still, few are willing to tolerate high fees, particularly when performance lags and liquidity terms are restrictive. Despite these recent headwinds, hedge funds continue to serve as important portfolio diversifiers and are often viewed as a potential source of alpha for institutional and accredited investors alike.

Increased Due Diligence Requirements

Raising assets has never been easy, especially for managers who are just starting out. Unless a manager walks out with funding from the parent company, he faces a challenge getting visibility and getting in front of the right investors early on.

People who have been in the industry for some time will remember when raising assets was easier. There was a flow, a shorter sales cycle, and shorter due diligence. Money was coming in with ease. You only needed to perform better than your peers, and the money would be there.

What was possible to accomplish in a few months prior to the 2008 economic crisis now takes over eighteen months to complete. Over time, attracting and maintaining investors' interest became much more difficult. Background checks became mandatory, and a double layer of references became the new standard in the industry. The amount of due diligence increased substantially, as did the anticipated level of transparency. In the past ten years, competition for the same dollar of investment has reached new heights.

The COVID crisis has recently sparked a brand-new set of obstacles for investment managers to successfully pass due diligence. Throughout 2020 and 2021, investors engaged in internal and public debates about the level of granularity necessary for new online due diligence to substitute for in-person meetings effectively as COVID raged. Due to the inability to convene in person, meetings were moved online to Zoom calls and webinars. This new obstacle increased the strain on managers to provide well thought out, well organized, and well-presented messaging for the funds they manage.

I remember attending the Endowment and Foundation Conference in Zurich shortly after the 2008 financial crisis. The conversations carried a sense of caution and reflection. Many allocators were reassessing how they approached manager selection and due diligence. During one panel, a group of CIOs discussed how their evaluation criteria had shifted. It was not just about performance anymore, it was also about trust, transparency, and how a manager handled pressure.

One CIO, speaking plainly from the stage, made a comment that stayed with me: "If I do not feel like having a beer with the fund manager, I just had a meeting with, I am not investing with him." The audience chuckled, but the point landed. Personal connection had become a real factor in decision making. After everything that had happened, allocators were placing more weight on character, communication, and whether they genuinely felt comfortable with the person behind the strategy. It was a simple reminder, relationships matter, often as much as the numbers.

Gap in Perception:
Investors vs. Hedge Fund Managers

Across countless hedge fund presentations, the way managers articulate their value to end investors tends to sound remarkably similar, at least to anyone who has reviewed many of them. Managers use standardized, cookie cutter methods or expressions to describe what they bring to the table. These claims are conveyed in broad and fundamental terms such as "teamwork," "unique investment process," "favorable risk adjusted returns," and "transparency."

Although valid and true, they are not supported by additional evidence. They also fail to emphasize how these statements differentiate the company from its competitors. It became exceedingly challenging to distinguish managers from one another and determine their true value proposition.

The brand consulting firm DeSantis Breindel conducted an industry survey in 2019. They interviewed 66 asset managers, forty consultants, and thirty-nine institutional investors to determine the significance of branding in the asset management industry

Seventy seven percent of asset managers responded affirmatively when asked whether they effectively differentiated themselves in the market. However, neither consultants nor allocators shared this viewpoint. Neither of them believed that asset managers successfully convey their value proposition.

Without knowing a manager's well defined and distinctive added value, investors are forced to spend more time attempting to comprehend the manager's goals and what sets them apart. As the key message becomes submerged in a sea of less pertinent information about the fund, investors frequently abandon the review.

Branding Concept in Asset Management

In comparison to other industries, the asset management industry adopted branding much later. In recent years, the importance of branding has increased significantly. Digital media and marketing development brought the branding concept to the forefront, it be-came a buzzword for corporations and businesses, and branding found implementation in personal marketing and promotion.

Exclusivity Delayed Branding

Over the years, hedge funds have found investors primarily through word of mouth and personal recommendations. The managers did not market to a wider audience.

Then, years of underperformance occurred. In an effort to recruit more investors and make their offering more appealing, minimum investments were reduced from 1 million dollars to 500,000 dollars and then even to 100,000 dollars. The entire asset management industry went through democratization.

Consequently, hedge funds were able to approach a broader range of institutions seeking to raise assets, including wealth advisors and investment platforms. Over time, the profile of hedge fund investors shifted from an exclusive group of affluent individuals to retail investors. With this shift in demographics, hedge funds are practically constrained in their ability to develop new promotional strategies.

The culture of the asset management industry is naturally conservative. Successful funds are viewed as stable, dependable, and adaptable to change. People who manage them are focused on generating exceptional returns and mitigating risk. In conjunction with the growing popularity of digital communication and digital media, the question emerged of how to present the company and establish a successful brand.

Digital corporate footprints and digital branding have been in existence for some time. It was only a matter of time before the asset management industry was disrupted. The COVID crisis merely establishes a digital presence, and adapt rapidly.

Importance of Brand Recognition

Brand recognition breeds brand loyalty

After the financial crisis in 2008, investors essentially invested their money in the same funds as they had before 2008, according to research by Guido Bollinger, Ivan Guidotti, and Florent Pochon (2010). Institutional investors, pension funds, foundations, and endowments were primarily responsible for driving asset flows to hedge funds. Money was placed in well-established funds, which already had a solid infrastructure in place and better name recognition. Investors demanded a heightened emphasis on liquidity and announced a new set of requirements and processes for managers to adhere to; however, they remained loyal to the familiar names and brands they knew well.

Brand recognition contributes to asset-raising success

Nasdaq eVestment Alliance conducted a study in 2018 on brand recognition in the asset management industry using data submitted by managers currently reporting on their platform. The study focused on active equity and fixed income from the beginning of 2012 to the end of 2017 and analyzed the responses consultants provided during their manager searches. Only 2 percent of managers, according to the report, accomplish appropriate branding and name recognition. The report also reveals that large investment institutions were only marginally better at branding than smaller firms despite their greater resources and manpower.

Furthermore, the firms that invested in branding experienced 20.3 times more inflows compared to those with limited brand recognition, according to the report

Brand awareness contributes to brand equity

Developing a reputable brand is crucial. Research by branding experts at Qualtrics (2021) highlights that consumers are significantly more inclined to choose products from familiar brands over those they do not recognize. Moreover, when loyal customers encounter issues or mistakes, they tend to be far more forgiving if the brand has already earned their trust.

Throughout the book, I am referring to hedge funds, but almost identical methodology applies to other asset managers, private equity, venture funds, or long only strategies.

History of Hedge Fund Branding

The branding of hedge funds has evolved significantly over the years, reflecting changes in the industry and the broader financial markets.

Early Years (1940s-1960s):

The concept of hedge funds dates back to 1949, when Alfred Winslow Jones launched the first hedge fund (AIMA, 2008). Initially, hedge funds operated with little public awareness and had a straightforward brand. Early hedge funds often relied heavily on personal networks and referrals. They raised capital from wealthy individuals within their social and professional circles. Given the small size of the industry, word of mouth played a significant role in fundraising. Successful fund performance would often spread through networks, attracting new investors. At that time, hedge funds began organizing themselves as limited partnerships. This structure aligned the interests between fund managers and investors, aiding fundraising efforts.

Growth and Innovation (1970s-1980s):

During the 1970s and 1980s, hedge funds began diversifying their strategies beyond traditional equity hedging to include global macro, fixed income, and currency trading. Branding was centered around exclusivity, a sophisticated approach, and the promise of high returns uncorrelated with the stock market. During that time, institutional investors like pension funds and endowments were largely absent from the hedge fund investor base. The hedge fund industry was too young and unconventional for many institutions, which preferred more established investment vehicles. The hedge fund space was much less regulated in this period, offering greater flexibility to fund managers to create returns, but posing a higher risk for investors.

To raise assets, fund managers relied on personal meetings to pitch their funds to prospective investors. Some hedge fund managers participated in investment clubs or financial forums where they could discuss their strategies with potential investors. Other fund managers formed relationships with boutique brokerage firms that catered to wealthy clients. These firms were able to facilitate introductions and foster agreements with personal investors.

Growth and Popularization (1980–1990)

The 1980s marked a turning point for the hedge fund industry. Once a niche corner of finance, hedge funds began to gain visibility, propelled by the rise of high-profile managers such as George Soros and Julian Robertson. These figures became synonymous with their funds, establishing powerful personal brands rooted in distinct investment philosophies and publicized successes.

As hedge funds demonstrated consistent performance and built longer track records, they began attracting a broader investor base. Institutional allocators, including pension funds, endowments, and insurance companies, were drawn by the promise of diversification and non-correlated returns. Their increasing interest was supported by the growing influence of investment consultants who began endorsing hedge funds as viable portfolio components.

Performance during periods of market volatility further cemented hedge funds' appeal. Events like the 1987 stock market crash showcased the ability of certain strategies to generate returns when traditional investments faltered. This reinforced hedge funds' reputation as sophisticated tools for managing downside risk.

The industry also witnessed a broadening of strategies. Managers moved beyond the traditional long short equity model, embracing global macro, distressed debt, arbitrage, and other alternative approaches. These offerings enabled greater alignment with varied investor needs and risk appetites, while positioning hedge funds as flexible, solutions-oriented vehicles. To support this evolution, hedge funds began formalizing their capital raising efforts. Dedicated marketing professionals were hired, investor communications were refined, and strategic branding became more deliberate. Industry conferences and seminars emerged as critical venues for showcasing track records and engaging prospects.

Another key development during this period was the rise of fund of funds. These pooled vehicles offered diversified exposure to hedge funds and opened access to investors who may have lacked the capital or experience to invest directly.

This innovation further democratized the hedge fund space and fueled its expansion.

Though still lightly regulated, hedge funds began operating under greater scrutiny, particularly around disclosures and marketing practices. By targeting accredited investors and aligning with emerging regulatory norms, many firms gained legitimacy and trust.

The prevailing "2 and 20" fee structure, 2 percent management fee and 20 percent performance fee, remained attractive amid strong returns, justifying premium pricing in the eyes of many investors. Capital raising also benefited from expanding distribution networks. Traditional relationship building persisted, but now included financial advisors, wealth managers, and institutional gatekeepers. Placement agents emerged as influential intermediaries, leveraging deep industry connections to match funds with appropriate capital sources.

Institutionalization (1990s-2000s)

The 1990s marked a significant milestone in the history of hedge funds. At that time, we saw exponential growth in the hedge fund industry, driven by high profile successes and increased institutional interest. Branding became more prominent, focusing on thought leadership, innovation, and the mystique of elite financial talent. Star managers gained celebrity like status. Hedge funds started adopting formal names, logos, and marketing materials to differentiate themselves. Performance track records became essential components of branding as funds sought to attract more sophisticated investors.

During the 1990s and early 2000s, the hedge fund industry underwent substantial changes as it matured and institutional investment grew. This period was marked by significant professionalization, increased regulatory scrutiny, and an explosion in assets under management. Large institutional investors like pension funds, endowments, and sovereign wealth funds began allocating substantial portions of their portfolios to hedge funds, seeking diversification and enhanced returns. Hedge funds often developed customized investment vehicles and separate accounts to meet institutional investors' specific needs and mandates.

Hedge funds built sophisticated marketing and sales teams to reach institutional investors systematically through well-organized campaigns. Participation in industry conferences and dedicated events targeting institutional investors became crucial for networking and showcasing fund capabilities.

Investment consultants played a key role in connecting hedge-funds with institutional capital, offering advice on allocation and performing due diligence. Professional placement agents were employed to facilitate the fundraising process, relying on their extensive networks to introduce funds to potential investors.

Hedge funds continually developed new strategies and products to cater to evolving market conditions and investor preferences. This included offering more sophisticated risk management tools and diversified strategies such as quantitative and multi strategy approaches. Funds differentiated by offering unique approaches, including sector specific, geographic focused, or innovative thematic investments.

Institutional investors demanded greater transparency and regular, detailed reporting on fund activities, performance, and risk metrics. Although hedge funds were relatively lightly regulated compared to other financial entities, they still adhered to increased regulatory requirements, which reassured investors.

The growth of fund of funds allowed smaller investors and institutions to gain diversified exposure to hedge funds, further increasing asset inflows into the industry. Fund of funds provided diversification benefits and comprehensive due diligence, which appealed to institutional investors.

Established funds with strong historical performance attracted significant interest. The ability to hedge risk and generate alpha during market disruptions made hedge funds attractive. Funds began to use performance benchmarks to communicate their relative success to potential investors.

Funds invested in technology, administrative systems, and operational processes to support growth and meet institutional standards. Enhanced risk management frameworks became integral to appealing to risk conscious institutional investors. At that time, hedge funds expanded their geographic reach, tapping into global markets for both investment opportunities and capital raising. Many larger funds opened offices in financial hubs around the world to broaden their investor base and enhance local market intelligence.

The period of institutional investment and professionalization in the 1990s and 2000s solidified the role of hedge funds as a core component of diversified investment portfolios. By adopting professional practices, embracing transparency, and developing innovative strategies, hedge funds successfully attracted a wider array of investors, significantly increasing their assets under management.

The 2008 Financial Crisis

The crisis was a pivotal moment for the hedge fund industry. Many funds faced significant losses, leading to increased scrutiny and regulatory changes. Branding shifted to transparency and risk management, with funds emphasizing robust risk controls and compliance to rebuild trust with investors.

Despite the challenging environment, some funds managed to navigate the crisis and emerge more assertive, while others faced considerable difficulties. Many investors sought liquidity during the financial turmoil, leading to significant redemption pressures on hedge funds. This was particularly challenging for funds with illiquid or hard to sell assets. Some funds suspended redemptions and put gates to manage redemption requests, which in some cases eroded investor trust.

Although some hedge funds demonstrated resilience and delivered positive returns, many experienced significant losses due to market volatility, leading to scrutiny over their purported risk management capabilities. As markets were reeling, there was an initial capital shift away from hedge funds toward perceived safer investments.

Hedge funds began heavily emphasizing their risk management frameworks as a core element of their strategy to reassure investors of their ability to handle market volatility. Greater transparency about risk exposure and investment processes became a central selling point to regain and attract investor confidence.

Some funds adjusted their fee structures to be more investor friendly, including lower management fees and more performance-based incentives. The use of hurdle rates and high watermark clauses became more prevalent, aligning manager compensation with performance to protect investor interests.

Fund managers increased the frequency and depth of communication with investors, providing detailed updates on fund positioning, performance, and market views. Personal interactions, meetings, and open dialogues were key to rebuilding trust and maintaining relationships with investors.

Hedge funds introduced innovative strategies to capture opportunities arising from market dislocations, such as distressed asset investing, credit arbitrage, and global macro strategies. There was a renewed focus on delivering non correlated returns to diversify investor portfolios effectively against systematic risks

At that time, hedge funds also strengthened their operational infrastructures to meet institutional standards and alleviate investor concerns about operational risks. As regulations like the Dodd Frank Act were enacted, funds improved their compliance practices to enhance their credibility with institutional investors.

The use of placement agents and consultants became more pronounced as funds sought to access a broader network of institutional investors and navigate complex regulatory landscapes. Collaborations with investment consultants were crucial for funds seeking to be included in institutional investment mandates.

Funds emphasized liquidity provisions to assure investors they could access their capital more readily, responding to the redemption challenges experienced during the crisis. Hedge funds offered separately managed accounts and customized solutions that aligned more closely with specific institutional needs, providing investors with more control and transparency.

Evolution in Digital Media (2010s-present)

With the rise of digital marketing and social media, hedge funds began to adopt more modern branding strategies. There was a greater emphasis on online presence, content marketing, and investor education. Funds started to leverage technology and data driven narratives to enhance their brand stories.

In the period from the 2010s to the present, the hedge fund industry has experienced significant changes due to the evolution of digital media, increased regulatory scrutiny, and the diversification of investment strategies. These factors have shaped how hedge funds raise assets, attract investors, and maintain relationships.

Hedge funds increasingly developed sophisticated websites and utilized social media platforms like LinkedIn for branding and outreach, enhancing their visibility and engagement with potential investors. Many funds created and shared insightful content using the latest technologies of artificial intelligence such as market analyses, research reports, and thought leadership articles to establish expertise and build trust with investors.

Webinars and virtual meetings became mainstream for investor presentations and due diligence processes, allowing funds to reach a global audience cost effectively. Funds adopted digital platforms to give investors real time access to reports, performance data, and updates, improving transparency and communication.

By employing data analytics, hedge funds tailored their marketing strategies to target specific investor segments more effectively based on preferences and behaviors. Funds strived to provide a personalized experience through tailored communication and investment offerings, enhancing investor satisfaction and retention.

Adopting regulatory technology solutions helped hedge funds efficiently comply with complex regulations, which built confidence with institutional investors through robust compliance systems. Enhanced compliance with digital communication guidelines set forth by entities like the SEC and FINRA ensured that funds could market themselves while adhering to legal requirements.

The introduction of structures such as interval funds and liquid alternatives provided retail investors with access to hedge fund strategies, expanding the potential investor base. Hedge funds increasingly focused on thematic investments and environmental, social, and governance strategies, appealing to socially conscious investors.

Funds used platforms that connect managers with potential investors, facilitating more structured and accessible networking and capital raising. Collaborations with fintech companies enabled hedge funds to leverage technological advancements in trading, data management, and investor relations.

After 2008, there has been a shift towards clearly articulating the value proposition of hedge fund investments, emphasizing risk adjusted returns, alpha generation, and diversification benefits. With more investment options available, hedge funds compete by demonstrating superior performance, unique strategies, or niche expertise.

Hedge funds increasingly targeted family offices and registered investment advisors, offering bespoke solutions and co investment opportunities. Although less conventional, some funds explored blockchain technology for raising capital and managing investor relationships, as well as crowdfunding platforms tailored for accredited investors.

Leveraging digital platforms, hedge funds extended their reach globally, attracting capital from international investors by showcasing their track records and strategic insights.

By embracing digital tools and strategies, hedge funds have enhanced their ability to reach a wider audience, offer greater transparency, and engage in more personalized investor relationships, which fostered growth in the modern investment landscape. Today, there is a greater emphasis on technology, sustainability, environmental, social and governance "ESG" considerations, and investor engagement. Branding now often highlights agility, data driven strategies, and personalized client service.

CHAPTER TWO

The Essence of Brand
Why Branding Matters

If you do not define your story, others will define it for you.

A brand is a comprehensive perception of a product or service based on its functionality, the problems it solves, the emotional experience it provides, the values and purpose it represents, it represents, and the relationship it fosters.

Some people confuse a brand with a company name, the logo, colors, or design of a business card. These are brand expressions that communicate to users the brand's characteristics. Branding is not an intangible, illusory phenomenon that occurs as a byproduct of doing business and has only a minor impact on profitability and success, it is the exact opposite. Product and service perceptions can be defined and created on purpose.

Long-term business success comes from a clear understanding of the value we offer, and the discipline to deliver it consistently.

In our personal lives, we have meaningful control over how others perceive us, and we can shape that perception through what we say, what we do, and what we consistently reinforce.

It is our responsibility to communicate our values and what is important to us. People will notice and associate these values with us once we make them an integral part of who we are, the same is true in the business world.

We can develop a set of values, character, organizational purpose, and a comprehensive picture of what we stand for proactively. Consistent communication of these values will help to solidify an organization's image. Over time, people will begin to associate these values with you and your company, defining their relation-ship with you.

If there is no intentional branding, the company is open to misinterpretation. The firm's intentions could be misunderstood. The desired reputation and image are at risk of being tarnished with little control and even less power to repair them. If we do not intentionally work on branding, investors and customers will form their own opinions about the company and its values. Good business relationships, like good personal relationships, are built on trust. To build trust, we need consistency. Branding creates conditions for that consistency.

We work on branding to improve people's perceptions of our organization, our work, our values, and the goal we strive for. Proactively defining what distinguishes us and what we strive to deliver consistently will shape others' perceptions. In the long run, we will benefit from this proactive approach.

The intersection of what investors experience and what we put out as who we are effectively determines a brand's success.

Both of these things must be in sync. The greater the alignment of these two factors, the more authentic and long lasting a brand will be.

With the deliberate creation of a brand, we put everything we are upfront and let go of everything we are not. That is extremely liberating. At any given time, we do not have solutions for everyone and everything, rather, we strive to focus on a select set of solutions and serve a certain market segment. Everything else takes a backseat.

Branding facilitates the free flow of business and relationships. It reminds me of the resonance law in physics. When one object vibrates at a certain natural frequency, it can cause another object with the same natural frequency to begin vibrating as well. This phenomenon, known as resonance, leads to amplification. In nature and human systems alike, when something emits a consistent, authentic signal, whether it is a sound, a message, or a brand identity, others that are attuned to the same frequency will naturally resonate with it, amplifying its impact, reach, and influence. Similarly, the more we define what we have to offer the world, the more likely it is that we will connect with the right people and investors, and the greater probability that the fund raising will be successful.

On February 17, 2021, Ray Dalio wrote on LinkedIn, "Spend lavishly on the time and energy you devote to getting in sync, because it is the best investment you can make".

Branding vs. Marketing and Sales

The distinction between branding, marketing, and sales may appear hazy when we consider their definitions and activities. Branding is everything that has to do with who we are, what we do, and how we communicate who we are. As previously stated, branding is primarily responsible for defining our culture, the values we cherish, and how others perceive and interact with us.

Marketing, on the other hand, entails a series of tactical and strategic activities that include communicating the brand's message, defining the target market, identifying target investors, and defining ways to communicate that message. It defines the four Ps of marketing: product, price, place, and promotion. It has also recently added two more Ps, participation and purpose, product positioning in comparison to competitors, and pricing in relation to the added value provided.

Sales initiates and tracks contact with investors. It generates reports and offers assistance and information flow until the final allocation is made. It ultimately uses all of the findings and outcomes of branding and marketing efforts to connect and bond with the end-user, your investors. Marketing and sales activities that are successful invariably contribute to the brand's value and brand awareness in the marketplace.

Firm Awareness vs. Product Awareness: Building Reputation and Visibility

Asset management and investment advisory services are examples of professional service brands. According to branding expert Hinge, the success of professional service brands is dependent on reputation and

visibility (Hinge Marketing, 2022). For clarity, let us go over these terms.

The most reputable firms are the ones that keep high standards of performance and investor services over the years. Large investments, as we all know, go to fund managers who have earned investors' trust by keeping their reputation intact. The term reputation has two aspects, general reputation and reputation as an expert. When we hear someone say, "They are a good firm" or "great guys to work with," we are talking about general reputation. It revolves around everything and anything related to the firm itself. You might be well known for your expertise in certain aspects of the business, the strategy you focus on, geographic exposure, or asset class. Expertise takes time to build, and it takes deliberate effort to promote the firm.

"The way to gain a good reputation is to endeavor to be what you desire to appear." *Socrates, Lives and Opinions, 3rd century.*

Visibility, on the other hand, asks how well-known the firm is to its target investors, if the firm is in front of the appropriate investors for its strategy and fund size, and if the firm is maximizing ways to access investors' attention.

Visibility comes two-fold, on the company and product levels. The fund manager provides professional expert services as an investment advisor. The investment firm is evaluated on the merits of the quality of services, honesty, transparency in communication with its clients and with third parties they work with. It is also evaluated based on the level of expertise and sophistication, the backgrounds and qualifications of team members, and the strength of partners and alliances.

However, product visibility is directly compared with alternative products in the marketplace vis a vis performance targets, investment philosophy, functionality, hedging features, and statistics. Investors aim to learn how compatible your strategy is with other strategies in their portfolio. They would like to know the ultimate functionality your strategy provides vis a vis other investment options.

It is essential to be aware early of these two levels of branding. They are two wheels turning simultaneously and in sync to create a complete and coherent story about the organization and the value it brings to the marketplace. It is wrong to assume that product is a brand. Lindsay Pedersen, a branding expert, argues that the product is an essential part of the brand promise (Pedersen, 2019).

Visibility is a sensitive concept and should be handled with care. If all other aspects of the business are optimized, better visibility brings higher awareness of investment services and fund solutions. Ideally, visibility is intentionally built to reach the attention of select target investors.

At times, however, visibility could be a sword with two blades. High visibility and brand awareness can have the opposite effect. If a firm goes through challenging times of negative performance, or if it is dealing with reputational challenges or the departure of key personnel, its high brand visibility has a much more significant contra effect than its benefits. To be exact, there were 1.7 times higher outflows compared to the comparable inflows according to the eVestment Alliance (2021) study. Many examples of companies facing ethical, legal, or compliance issues in the media, experienced outflows following the events. The effect of negative bias remains present for some time, and it is not easy to correct in most cases.

eVestment Alliance finds that having more products does not necessarily mean stronger brand recognition. Many managers create two or three strategies on day one, strategies that are marginally different from one another. They end up directly competing for the same investor dollar and, over time, neither achieves proper funding. Investors recognize this. According to the eVestment report, products managed is not a key driver in investor searches when evaluating a manager. For example, the endowment of an Ivy League university, a very active allocator to hedge strategies and alternatives, does not invest in startup managers with more than one strategy. They argue that a manager does not believe in the flagship strategy if he has a few strategies to rely on in case the flagship fund does not succeed. The bottom line is to focus on what you are good at and be consistent.

Let us look at the relationship between firm and product awareness. The balance between the two matters. Research suggests that firms with high product awareness and low firm awareness do not significantly attract investors. If a fund is performing very well, and the investor community is unaware of the firm and who they are, the likelihood of high inflows is low.

The same holds true for the opposite. If investors know the firm very well but are unaware of the uniqueness of its offering, inflows will not come. In other words, wellknown firms with high firm awareness and no product awareness do not generate inflows. This speaks volumes about what investors find essential when selecting a manager. Only the right combination of firm and product awareness generates notable results, measured by higher inflows.

According to the study, if the mix of firm and product awareness is not optimal either way, larger firms experience higher volatility of inflows and outflows than small firms. This balance cannot be achieved overnight. Building a reputation and tracking it takes time. However, it is accomplished step by step, incrementally every day, with every interaction with the investor community.

Regarding what to do first, establishing expertise and general reputation comes first. Creating strong visibility follows and reinforces it into a strong and successful brand. Firms with strong reputation and high visibility are better positioned to build durable brands.

29

CHAPTER THREE

The Architecture of a Brand

Establishing the Truth Before Designing the Brand

Every credible brand begins with an honest assessment of reality. Before positioning is refined or narratives are shaped, a firm must understand how it is perceived, how it operates in practice, and how those actions are interpreted by investors.

When brand creation is approached with discipline, it begins with audit and research. For a portfolio manager, this first step is a structured self-examination of the investment strategy, the organization that supports it, and the value the firm delivers to investors over time.

The purpose of this initial step is clarity. Before a brand can be articulated, it must be understood, accurately and without self-reference. Allocators allocate capital to evidence, behavior, and consistency. A credible brand therefore emerges only when the manager has subjected the firm to the same level of scrutiny an allocator will ultimately apply.

From an allocator's perspective, diligence is not intended to validate strengths, but to identify misalignment. They are far less concerned with whether a manager can tell a compelling story than with whether that story is aligned with observable outcomes.

"Most managers do not fail because they lack strengths. They fail because they do not understand which strengths investors actually perceive." - *Senior Investment Officer, Public Pension Fund*

Quantitative vs. Qualitative Assessment

In brand creation, audit and research have two essential dimensions: quantitative and qualitative. Both are foundational. Neither is sufficient in isolation.

The quantitative dimension establishes how the strategy behaves. Performance is examined not simply in terms of returns, but through volatility, drawdowns, recovery dynamics, correlation characteristics, capacity constraints, and resilience across market regimes. Risk metrics, portfolio concentration, liquidity profiles, and operational structure all contribute to an allocator's assessment of reliability and portfolio fit.

The objective of this analysis is not to determine whether results are attractive in absolute terms. It is to determine whether they behave in a manner consistent with the strategy's stated intent, and whether that behavior contributes meaningfully to an investor's portfolio.

The qualitative dimension addresses perception, credibility, and trust. It examines how the firm is understood by internal stakeholders, existing investors, prospective allocators, consultants, and counterparties. These perspectives frequently diverge from a manager's internal view of the organization.

The objective here is coherence. Branding loses effectiveness when managers emphasize attributes they believe to be distinctive but that investors either do not recognize or do not value. Audit and research surface these discrepancies early, before they become embedded in positioning that lacks credibility.

Qualitative research must also encompass communication behavior. This includes reviewing how the firm has communicated during periods of underperformance, how errors were acknowledged and explained, and whether messaging evolved appropriately as conditions changed. Allocators often place greater weight on these periods than on extended intervals of strong performance.

"I learn more about a manager in a difficult quarter than in a strong year.", *Chief Investment Officer, Family Office*

Competitive and Portfolio Context

Audit and research extend beyond the organization itself. Allocators never evaluate managers in isolation, and neither should portfolio managers engaged in brand creation. Competitive and portfolio context are essential. This includes understanding how the strategy compares to peers and substitutes, where overlap may diminish relevance, and where differentiation may be structurally constrained.

Equally important is an understanding of allocator constraints. Investment committees operate within defined policy limits, liquidity requirements, governance frameworks, and, in some cases, political considerations. A strategy may be theoretically compelling yet operationally impractical. Research that fails to account for these constraints produces positioning that resonates conceptually but fails to translate into allocation.

As the first step in brand creation, audit and research establish the conditions for credibility. They clarify what the firm genuinely offers, where it adds value, and where further discipline or development is required. Only once this reality is understood does brand design become meaningful.

Once this internal assessment is complete, the perspective must shift outward to how allocators evaluate, filter, and ultimately underwrite these findings.

Inside the Allocator's Mind

Portfolio Construction Under Modern Constraints

In the world of institutional investing, performance is only one piece of the puzzle. The real mandate allocators face is far more nuanced; they are tasked with building resilient, goal-aligned portfolios that can endure volatility, deliver on long-term promises, and navigate across multiple constraints such as liquidity, governance, mission, and optics.

Whether it is a university endowment seeking to fund scholarships in perpetuity, a public pension managing obligations for millions of retirees, or a foundation working toward social impact, every allocator is an architect, designing not just for returns but for resilience, flexibility, and narrative clarity. This architecture is under pressure like never before.

"The job is not to find the best performing manager; it is to build the best performing portfolio." - *Chief Investment Officer, 15-billion-dollar University Endowment; SEI, Governance Best Practices for Endowments and Foundations, 2023*

The traditional 60/40 portfolio, a staple for decades, is no longer fit for purpose. With bond yields compressed and equity markets both expensive and volatile, the expected return from a classic asset mix falls short of institutional return hurdles, which typically range between 6.5 percent to 8 percent. At the same time, risks have become more complex and interconnected. Inflation shocks, geopolitical realignments, liquidity crunches, and the rising correlation between asset classes challenge the core assumptions of modern portfolio theory.

"We are not looking for heroes; we are looking for tools to help us build a better risk adjusted portfolio." - *Director of Investments, 6-billion-dollar Healthcare System; eVestment, Hedge Fund Investor Survey, Q2 2023*

In this environment, hedge fund managers are uniquely positioned to add value, but only if they understand what allocators are truly solving for. It is not about offering the highest Sharpe ratio or the most exciting trade idea, it is about understanding how a strategy contributes to the construction of a stronger, more adaptable portfolio.

Diversification That Holds in Crisis

On the surface, most institutional portfolios look diversified. However, in moments of stress, underlying correlations spike. This correlation breakdown has caught many institutions off guard. The 2008 financial crisis was a wake-up call, and the liquidity scramble of the first quarter of 2020 during COVID was another. In 2022, when inflation surged and both stocks and bonds collapsed simultaneously, many allocators faced their worst drawdowns in decades. (Preqin, Global Alternatives Report 2023)

These moments crystallized a truth most allocators now live by, diversification is not what works in calm markets, it is what holds up under pressure.

"Do not show me a pretty Sharpe ratio, show me what you did when everything else was bleeding." - *Portfolio Manager, 11-billion dollar Foundation; AIMA and CAIA, Due Diligence Guide for Institutional Investors, 2023*

Hedge funds that offer returns that are statistically independent or uncorrelated with broader market movements can provide what traditional markets cannot, resilience when it matters most.

However, allocators do not want a strategy that simply claims low correlation. They want to understand why that correlation holds, how the return is generated, and what scenarios may cause it to break. They are not just buying alpha; they are buying behavior under stress. (AIMA and CAIA, Due Diligence Guide for Institutional Investors, 2023)

Liquidity Budgeting and Dry Powder

Institutional portfolios are increasingly divided into liquidity tiers. Private markets, such as private equity, infrastructure, and venture capital, offer higher returns on paper, yet they come at the cost of multi-year capital lockups. Over time, these illiquid assets often outperform and grow disproportionately within the portfolio, leaving allocators overexposed and unable to rebalance when needed.

This liquidity creep creates a quiet yet powerful portfolio construction challenge.

"I love my private equity portfolio, but I cannot eat IRR. I need managers who help me stay nimble." - *Chief Investment Officer, 4-billion-dollar Public Pension; Bain and Company, Global Private Equity Report 2024*

In response, there is growing demand for semi-liquid and liquid alternatives, hedge fund strategies that can deliver meaningful returns while preserving optionality. Monthly and quarterly liquidity are no longer liabilities; they are assets in themselves. Managers who can operate effectively within these liquidity windows without compromising alpha are solving a critical problem for modern allocators.

Hidden Crowding and Factor Exposure

Another challenge in portfolio construction is factor overlap. Allocators often discover, too late, that their portfolio contains multiple strategies with hidden exposure to the same market risks. A long short equity fund, a smart beta ETF, and an outsourced CIO tactical sleeve may all be unknowingly betting on United States technology momentum or long duration.

> "We already own the S&P500 six different ways. What do you actually add?" - *Investment Committee Member, Ivy League Endowmenti Connections Conference; Allocator Panel on Differentiation in Manager Selection, New York, 2023*

This is why allocators increasingly ask hedge fund managers to go beyond correlation tables and explain their factor footprint. What risks are you long or short? How do your positions respond to macro shocks? What is your exposure to duration, inflation, or credit?

Winning hedge funds demonstrate idiosyncrasy not only in holdings but in process, decision making, and portfolio construction discipline.

Explaining Risk to the Board

Even the most compelling strategy must survive the investment committee filter.

Today's Chief Investment Officers must answer not only to internal stakeholders, but also to external watchdogs, consultants, auditors, and, especially in the public sector, taxpayers and politicians. Allocations must align with mission, withstand scrutiny, and be grounded in good governance.

> "If I cannot explain your strategy in two minutes, I cannot own it."
> *- Deputy Chief Investment Officer, 9-billion-dollar Religious Organization; AIMA, Operational Due Diligence for Allocators, Workshop Series 2023*

This is a major pain point. Many technically sophisticated managers lose mandates not because of performance but because they fail the explainability test. Complexity is not a virtue in the boardroom. Hedge funds must now offer both intellectual depth and narrative clarity.

Building for the Whole Portfolio

Ultimately, the allocator's job is not to assemble a list of good managers, it is to build a functioning portfolio ecosystem, one that is resilient, flexible, aligned with long term goals, and capable of surviving the next unknown.

The hedge fund manager of the future must understand this. The role extends beyond product delivery. It is about solving liquidity mismatches, mitigating factor crowding and correlation risk, navigating governance constraints, and closing return gaps. In that role, the manager becomes a portfolio partner.

With an understanding of how allocators think and decide, attention can now turn to how differentiation is recognized through that same lens.

Differentiation Through the Allocator's Lens

In a crowded investment landscape, most managers view their strategy as differentiated. Allocators, looking across hundreds of opportunities, arrive at a far narrower conclusion.

This gap rarely reflects a lack of brilliance or effort. It usually stems from confusion about how differentiation is formed and whose judgment ultimately determines it. Managers look at differentiation through their own process and perspective. Allocators judge it by its impact on the overall portfolio

For allocators, differentiation begins with necessity. Every strategy is evaluated in the context of what already exists in the portfolio, the risks already taken, and the objectives that still need to be met. A new allocation earns attention only when it contributes something distinct to that mix. Compelling narratives, strong opinions, and even attractive returns carry little weight unless the strategy improves the portfolio as a whole.

Viewing differentiation through the allocator's lens shifts attention to durability. Certain characteristics continue to matter when conditions change—when markets reverse, correlations rise, liquidity tightens, and familiar explanations lose relevance. Strategies that remain useful in those environments stand out quickly. Their value comes from how they behave, how they absorb stress, and how consistently they serve their intended role.

Allocators assess differentiation by watching behavior over time. They study how a strategy responds during difficult periods, how it interacts with other holdings, and how transparent its weaknesses are. Predictable limitations tend to be easier to manage than unexpected surprises. Clear structure, disciplined execution, and steady decision-making matter more than complexity or originality.

This perspective narrows the field. Many qualities managers highlight, sophisticated models, broad mandates, elaborate frameworks, tend to lose importance under sustained scrutiny. What continues to resonate are a small number of durable attributes: structural advantages that resist replication, clearly defined boundaries that guide behavior, decision processes that remain intact under pressure, and incentive structures that reinforce long-term stewardship.

Differentiation also depends on context. A strategy's value changes depending on what an allocator already owns. What strengthens one portfolio may duplicate risk in another. This is why allocators ask direct and sometimes uncomfortable questions: What breaks first? Where does this hurt us? What happens when it doesn't work? These questions help determine whether a strategy adds something distinct or simply adds more exposure to familiar risks.

Focusing on true differentiators changes the conversation. Attention moves away from describing the manager and toward understanding the contribution. Broad positioning gives way to specific relevance. Restraint becomes a strength. Strategies that endure tend to stand apart on a few dimensions rather than many, and those dimensions are clearly defined, intentionally chosen, and reinforced through consistent behavior.

The sections that follow make this evaluation explicit. Identifying true differentiators requires a disciplined look at structure, behavior, and decision-making, guided by the questions allocators ask when capital is exposed to real risk.

Managers who engage seriously with this process often emerge with fewer differentiators than they expected. The ones that remain, however, tend to be clearer, more defensible, and far more likely to endure.

How to Identify True Differentiators

True differentiation in asset management is rarely obvious and almost never accidental. In competitive markets, many strategies appear distinct during favorable conditions, yet few remain meaningfully

differentiated when performance compresses, markets reverse, or familiar narratives lose credibility. What allocators ultimately reward is not novelty, but durability.

Differentiators are revealed through evidence, behavior, and constraint, most clearly when conditions are least forgiving.

Step One:

Consider Performance as Structure, Not Magnitude

Allocators analyze *how performance behaves* rather than what it delivers. Their attention centers on:

- How returns evolve across market regimes
- The depth, duration, and recovery profile of drawdowns
- Whether results reflect consistency of process or dependence on specific conditions or factors

These elements reveal whether performance is the outcome of design or circumstance.

How to do it: Begin by separating what performance looks like from why it behaves the way it does. Map returns across different environments, examine drawdown behavior in detail, and decompose results to isolate true drivers of return. The goal is not to eliminate periods of underperformance, but to understand them.

Key questions to ask:
- In which environments does the strategy perform as designed, and why?
- Where does it underperform, and what trade-offs explain that behavior?
- How does the strategy behave during stress, volatility, or liquidity contraction?
- How predictable and disciplined is recovery following drawdowns?

> **Allocator reality check:**
> - Performance remains logically consistent if market conditions reverse
> - Returns can be explained without relying on favorable narratives
> - Results withstand factor attribution and beta decomposition

If performance cannot be structurally explained, it cannot differentiate.

Step Two:
Define Structural Alpha and Replication Barriers

Durable alpha rarely stems from superior forecasts. More often, it is rooted in structural advantages such as:

- Restricted access to markets or opportunities
- Execution capabilities others lack
- Operational or technological infrastructure
- Regulatory, legal, or jurisdictional complexity

These frictions determine who can participate, and who cannot.

How to do it: Identify precisely where the strategy benefits from constraint or complexity, then test whether those advantages survive scale, competition, and institutional replication. The emphasis should be on what prevents others from doing the same thing, not on what makes the strategy sound compelling.

Key questions to ask:
- What limits participation by other managers?
- What would fail if a large institution attempted replication?
- Which elements require specialized infrastructure, permissions, or expertise?
- Does the edge persist as capital scales and markets evolve?

Allocator reality check:
- Alpha comes from execution or access, not prediction
- The edge survives increased efficiency and competition
- Replication requires meaningful infrastructure

Step Three:

Design Strategy Through Intentional Constraints

Allocators place significant weight on restraint. They focus on:

- Clearly defined investment universes
- Disciplined use of instruments and structures
- Explicit holding period and liquidity parameters
- Geographic and concentration boundaries

Constraints clarify intent.

How to do it: Explicitly define what the strategy does *not* do. Clarify exclusions, boundaries, and failure conditions. Constraint should be articulated as a feature, not a limitation.

Key questions to ask:
- What opportunities are always excluded?
- Where is the strategy intentionally narrow?
- Under what conditions would the strategy stop working?

Allocator reality check:
- The strategy says "no" more often than "yes"
- Failure conditions are explicit and realistic

Step Four:

Clarify the Decision-Making Architecture

Allocators invest in decision systems, not ideas. Their focus includes:

- Where authority resides
- How accountability is enforced
- How disagreement is resolved

How to do it: Make decision rights visible. Document how authority functions in practice, particularly during disagreement or stress.

Key questions to ask:
- Who has final decision authority?
- How are disagreements resolved in reality, not theory?
- When was a major decision reversed, and why?

Allocator reality check:
- Decision authority is clear and stable
- The process alters behavior, not just discussion

Step Five:

Demonstrate Risk Discipline Through Action

Risk discipline is evaluated through behavior. Allocators focus on:

- Actions that are explicitly prohibited
- Moments when exposure was reduced
- Upside that was intentionally sacrificed

How to do it: Identify concrete instances where risk rules overrode conviction. These moments define credibility.

Key questions to ask:
- What actions are explicitly prohibited, regardless of opportunity?
- When did risk constraints force difficult decisions?
- What upside was intentionally sacrificed?

Allocator reality check
- Risk rules meaningfully constrain conviction
- Risk management affects real-time decisions

Step Six:
Align Incentives to Reinforce Stewardship

Incentives reveal intent. Allocators examine:

- Fee behavior during weak performance
- Personal capital invested alongside clients
- Alignment with long-term outcomes

How to do it: Analyze how economics behave under stress, not just during growth. Incentives should reinforce stewardship rather than asset accumulation.

Key questions to ask:
- How do fees behave during periods of underperformance?
- How much personal capital is invested alongside clients?
- What behaviors does the structure discourage?

Allocator reality check
- Economics reward managing well, not managing more.

Step Seven:
Prove Institutional Readiness Under Stress

Trust is built when performance is challenged. Allocators focus on:
- Communication quality
- Transparency under pressure
- Investor behavior during drawdowns

How to do it: Review conduct during periods of stress. Outcomes matter less than behavior.

Key questions to ask:
- How did communication change during drawdowns?
- Were errors acknowledged and explained?
- Did investors add, hold, or redeem?

> **Allocator reality check:**
> - Transparency improves when conditions worsen
> - Investors maintain or increase exposure during stress

Step Eight:
Use Technology to Change Outcomes

Technology differentiates only when it alters decisions.

How to do it: Identify where technology improves judgment, timing, or execution, not presentation.

> **Key questions to ask:**
> - Which outcomes are materially better because of technology?
> - What degrades if technology disappears?

> **Allocator reality check**
> - Technology changes outcomes, not presentations

Step Nine:

Integrate ESG Only Where It Alters the Portfolio

Allocators focus on portfolio impact, not narrative.

How to do it: Trace ESG integration directly to investment decisions and risk outcomes.

Key questions to ask:
- Which investments exist because ESG is embedded?
- How does ESG alter risk, drawdowns, or capital preservation?

Allocator reality check:
- ESG affects portfolio construction, not reporting

Step Ten:

Build Adaptability Without Style Drift

Longevity depends on disciplined change.

How to do it: Document past adaptations and define future triggers for change.

Key questions to ask:
- Which edge has been abandoned, and why?
- What signals prompt adaptation?

Allocator reality check:
- Adaptation is pre-defined, not reactive

Managers who approach differentiation with this level of rigor identify fewer edges, but those edges are stronger, more defensible, and far more likely to endure.

52

CHAPTER FOUR

Brand Strategy and Positioning

Being understood is a competitive edge.

Brand Positioning

Brand positioning represents a strategic marketing concept that defines how a brand occupies a distinct place in the minds of its clients. It is a method of discovering unique propositions, differentiating from competitors, and creating undeniable value for the people and businesses served.

Unique Value Proposition

A true value proposition only becomes clear when three things are examined side by side: what investors actually need, what competitors already offer, and what your firm can deliver consistently and credibly. Investors are not searching for novelty for its own sake, they are searching for solutions to specific, recurring problems. Meanwhile, markets are crowded with firms that sound different but look remarkably similar, often differentiated more by language than by substance.

When these realities are confronted honestly, differentiation stops being a creative exercise and becomes a process of elimination. The work begins with everything investors hear in the market. From there, you strip away what everyone already says. Next, you remove what you cannot clearly demonstrate or sustain over time. What remains is not excess, it is focus. And that focus is your unique value proposition, your edge.

This discipline forces clarity in three critical areas: a deep understanding of what investors truly care about and what concerns them most; a precise articulation of the value you provide and why it is genuinely distinctive; and an honest assessment of who you compete with, why, and on what dimensions. Differentiation does not come from doing more. It comes from knowing exactly what to emphasize and what to leave out.

As Peter Thiel famously observed, *"If you are not a little different, you are invisible."* In the end, investors reward precision, not abundance.

Paradigm Shift: From Performance to Problem Solving

A familiar pattern often unfolds in the early life of a fund. After years of research and rigorous testing, a manager develops a strategy that performs as intended. A track record begins to form one, two, perhaps three years of results, and with it comes the excitement to share the story with prospective investors. Meetings are secured, conversations begin, and the focus quickly turns to performance. The manager

speaks passionately about what the fund can do yet rarely addresses what it is actually designed to solve. The discussion centers on returns, while the underlying problem the strategy is meant to address remains unspoken.

Performance matters, but it is only one element of a much larger decision-making framework. When meetings end, the manager often walks away hopeful, yet with little insight into the real objectives, constraints, or concerns of the investors across the table. Trust, like any meaningful connection, is built not through explanation alone, but through listening through understanding what the other party needs and how you can help meet that need.

Investors are far from a homogeneous group. Risk tolerance, return expectations, time horizons, and mandates vary widely. The objectives of an endowment may differ fundamentally from those of a family office, and even within the same category, investors can diverge significantly in style and priorities. Recognizing and understanding these differences is essential.

The work begins well before the meeting. Managers must invest time in learning how a prospective investor allocates capital, how long they commit it, what risks they are willing to bear, and what outcomes they seek. When working with a placement agent, this preparation is often strengthened by long-standing relationships and institutional knowledge. With proper preparation, the conversation shifts from a generic pitch to a focused dialogue shaped around the needs of the investor. Trust follows more naturally when investors feel understood and when the fund is positioned not just as a strategy, but as a solution.

Clarifying What Sets You Apart

Finding what differentiates you is also a journey of self-discovery. During this process, you may conclude that nothing has to be modified. This is simply a recognition and acceptance of what is already there, the state of the facts about who you are. Consider what qualities have led to your success thus far and what others admire about your work as a starting point.

However, in this process, you may discover new facts that lead you in a different direction. Do not be reluctant to make that adjustment. During my practice, I worked with a manager who initially intended to start a hedge fund, but after conducting an attribution study, he recognized that his long only carve out strategy outperformed the hedging strategy in comparison to their respective indices. In his case, shorting was not a strength. In the end, his long only carve out drew the attention of an institutional allocator. Investors do recognize quality. The challenge is to be completely open and flexible while striving for the best quality and service we can provide.

Focus with Intent

By narrowing the scope of services you provide, you will establish clear positioning against competitors and create a more memorable brand identity. A targeted solutions approach elevates customer trust and loyalty, results in stronger mutual relationships, and leads to better client satisfaction and ultimately higher client retention. It also has business advantages, it streamlines processes, allows focused resource allocation, and enables easier checks and balances.

As a starting point for building your narrow scope, you should capitalize on your most prominent strength.

There are a few places online where you can evaluate your personality, strengths and weaknesses, management style, and communication style. There are two which I found very useful, VIA Institute on Character, 2023, and Principles You by Ray Dalio personality test, 2022. I found them useful not only to learn more and confirm what I know about myself, but they also provide the ability to check compatibility among team members.

It is useful to list your technical skill inventory, specialized knowledge areas, and any unique methodologies or proprietary techniques you have used to achieve superior returns. A narrow scope of specialization can emerge from recurring themes in past successes, specialized problem types you have solved, or areas in which others consistently seek your advice.

Conducting an analysis of what is currently present in the marketplace as a solution can help you identify underserved niches and spot gaps in available expertise. While monitoring market trends and researching demand patterns, you can discover unique combinations of service and expertise that fit the needs of investors.

The narrow scope you select must be undeniably valuable to your clients. It should be easy to spot and easy to understand. It must be measurable and well documented. You can use different measures of efficiency, performance improvement, and value-added ratios to communicate these benefits in your marketing materials. Case studies, success stories, impact analysis, and comparison studies can be effective ways to present them.

Remember, focus creates clarity. Specialization builds authority. Narrow scope deepens impact.

Target Audience Definition

When you ask a manager, who can you serve, the instinctive answer is almost always the same: Everyone. Our strategy can benefit any portfolio. That may be true in theory, but it is a weak positioning choice in practice. A strategy does not solve every investor's problem equally well. It expresses certain performance characteristics, volatility profile, drawdown behavior, liquidity footprint, correlation tendencies, carry, convexity, factor exposures, that become most valuable in specific portfolio settings and specific market regimes. Your job is to identify where your strategy is most needed, not where it is merely acceptable.

Start with the data. When you examine the performance and risk attributes of your strategy, you will see patterns: environments where you protect capital, periods where you diversify, conditions where you produce asymmetric outcomes, and constraints you handle better than peers. Those patterns point directly to the investors who benefit most. The ideal investor is not the person who likes your story, it is the portfolio where your strategy becomes a solution.

The difficult part is choice. Defining an ideal investor requires the discipline to narrow the aperture and let go of the comforting idea that you can be everything to everyone. This is not about turning away capital; it is about deciding where you will spend your scarce time. Targeting means prioritizing which allocator types, portfolio roles, and use-cases you will build your narrative around, and which you will pursue only opportunistically.

There is also a practical reality for emerging managers: you keep the doors open. Early-stage firms often need flexibility to survive. But flexibility is not the same as vagueness. You can accept business from a range of investors while still having a sharply defined center of gravity, the segment where you win most often, retain clients longest, and build the strongest referrals. Clarity does not exclude you; it focuses you on the most profitable and repeatable segment of your market.

Competitive Analysis

It is not an easy task to get detailed information on hedge fund strategies. A lot of managers are not reporting to major databases. Their strategies predominantly stay confidential to repel any potential competition and preserve the uniqueness of the strategy. This is especially true for strategies with low barriers to entry. Yet efforts to find data will be well worth it. Tap your resources, call your prime broker, best investors, or administrators for their help, or purchase the data from the data providers to get the information you need.

This exercise of comparability is not something you have to perform very often. How many new hedge funds or strategies similar to yours are launched in a year? Not too many. So, giving it good attention initially will go a long way.

Complementarity vs. Substitution

In life, as in business, we are continuously looking for ways to differentiate ourselves from competitors, but we must also remain aware of how complementary we are to them. Your strategy might be complementary to the current holdings the investor already has in the portfolio. Assume an allocator has made prior investments in your competitor. You might be an excellent diversifier for their portfolio. Your strategy may complement the manager's strategy in which they have already invested. Discovering how complementary your strategy is to the investors' current holdings can help you identify ways to find your place in the investors' portfolio. A good practice would be to generate an internal report that compares your competitors' strategies to your own. You can share data with prospective investors during the meeting or call or opt not to present it at all.

While searching for the best solutions, investors will consider not only your direct competitors but also any other solution that can substitute the functionalities and elements of your strategy. Investors will take into consideration related mutual funds, ETFs, or long-only strategies.

You must always consider what other options investors could invest in to achieve the same or similar goals. According to the answer, analyze how you compare with all of them.

Sharpening your Edge

When we define who we are, we consequently communicate what we are not. The same stands for a brand. To achieve the highest visibility, it is important to create well-defined lines which distinguish where our brand stops and something else begins. Sharpening the edges and highlighting the differences from the next competitor brings clarity in the eyes of the investors, fortifies their trust, and facilitates their engagement with you.

"The essence of strategy is choosing what not to do." *Michael Porter, Competitive Strategy (1980)*

The best way to introduce the edge is to apply contrasting. By using traits which distinguish your strategy from the competitors, you can create contrast. The contrast can be used not only when describing how your strategy differs and where it adds the best value but also in other ways in which your clients experience the brand: professional vs. approachable, sophisticated vs. casual, innovative vs. traditional, technology vs. humanity, global vs. local, exclusive vs. inclusive, self-service vs. full-service, customized vs. standardized, and so on. Highlight your special capabilities, novel solutions, and different perspectives. All contrasts have to have clear purpose and meaning. They should be relevant to your client objectives and have sustainable execution.

Being Different but Relatable

"Invisible Influence" by Berger (2016) explains the concept of mere exposure. The book explains that we do show biases when we are exposed to something new. In order to accept the new, our brain has tendencies to associate new information with something familiar, something already known. If something is completely novel, it is harder to accept. Novel strategies should be anchored in attributes that are already familiar to the audience.

62

CHAPTER FIVE

Brand Expression and Narrative

What you choose to repeat becomes what you are believed to be

Brand Promise

A brand promise is simple: do what you said you would do, every time. Reaching that point requires restraint. Begin by looking at everything you offer and narrowing it to the outcome that matters most to the client and that you can deliver without exception. If an outcome depends on ideal conditions, heroic effort, or constant customization, it does not belong in your promise.

The promise must be defined in concrete terms. It should be clear what is delivered, when it is delivered, and what success looks like. Vague language creates flexibility for you but uncertainty for the client, and uncertainty erodes trust. Precision, by contrast, reduces perceived risk and sets expectations you can consistently meet.

Execution must then be aligned around protecting that promise. This means designing workflows, timelines, and decision-making processes that prioritize reliability over range. It also means declining work that would compromise delivery. Over time, consistent execution turns predictability into trust. Clients return, expand the relationship, and refer others not because of how ambitious your brand sounds, but because it is dependable.

Reason to believe

In her book Ironclad Branding Strategy, Pedersen (2019) shares with us that by defining your brand promise, you state what you are going to constantly deliver to the client. But to firmly set and fortify that statement in the minds of clients, you need to give them a reason to believe. It is proof why you will be able to deliver what you said you are going to do for them. It can be related to the resources you have, new models and proprietary technologies, or something else. The role of these reasons, as Lindsay said, is to support the brand promise.

For instance, if your promise is that you are going to deliver a small aberration in the stock prices between ADRs and GDRs and local shares in the Indian stock market, your reason to believe is the fact that your firm is the largest arbitrageur by volume in India with thirty traders trading around the clock for your portfolio. Another example, your promise is to deliver the unique alpha from small cap equities in a country specific strategy. Your reason to believe would be the fact that your firm has over one hundred analysts sitting in the local market and has meetings with the management of companies on a regular basis, and so on.

Ultimate award

Pedersen in her book also mentioned a tactic that communicates your brand value quite efficiently. You state what you are going to do for a client so they can afford to enjoy something that they care for or achieve something they strive to do. It is structured as, (brand promise) so that you can (ultimate award). For example, we focus on investments so that you can focus on managing the endowment. Or we focus on managing the downside risk so that you can have stable income and peace of mind. The most effective ultimate award is a desire of the clients which they do not particularly articulate but on some level care for deeply. To do this well, it is very helpful to know your potential investor well.

To summarize, the brand positioning has to be relevant, it must matter to your audience. It has to be easily recognizable and should set you apart from your competitors. Proper positioning will create higher credibility. It will foster a believable and authentic brand. The promises it makes should be well communicated and maintained over time.

Positioning can be viewed and communicated through several distinct lenses. It may be expressed through the features embedded in your methodology by highlighting what structurally differentiates your approach. It can be framed through benefits, focusing on the tangible value your service delivers to investors. Positioning can also be defined by implementation, clarifying where and when your offering is most effective, or by identifying the investors for whom it is best suited.

In addition, positioning may be shaped through pricing, whether by establishing a premium offering or signaling efficiency, and through quality, emphasizing depth of expertise, rigor, and a differentiated methodology. Each lens offers a different way to articulate relevance, but effective positioning requires choosing the angle that most clearly reinforces your core advantage rather than attempting to use them all at once.

The Drivers Behind the Organization

In its final form, the driving forces are communicated through North Star statements, definitions of vision, mission, and value. All three statements together define what value you bring to the table, what you care for, and map out the direction in which the organization is heading.

There are a lot of examples where these three statements are intertwined, not well articulated, and replaced with one another. Let us clarify them.

Mission answers the question of what the purpose of the firm is and what you are here to solve. Investment managers, while creating the statement, should focus on aspects of performance and client service and ensure it communicates commitment to generating superior returns and the ability to navigate diverse market environments.

Bridgewater Capital states on their website as their mission: "Our overriding objective is excellence. When we say excellence, we mean constant improvement. Our mission of understanding how the world's markets and economies work requires an extraordinary team, defined by the best individuals and the best portfolio of people, operating in an environment where we are uncompromising on our shared values of truth, integrity, determination, humility, and courage. This way of being is a self-reinforcing cycle that propels us forward through good and bad times and creates deep meaning in our work and relationships.

Example of Point72 mission statement: "Our mission is to be the industry's premier asset management firm through delivering superior risk-adjusted returns, adhering to the highest ethical standards and offering the greatest opportunities to the industry's brightest talent."

AQR Asset Management mission statement: "At the nexus of economics, behavioral finance, data and technology, AQR's evolution over two decades has been a continuous exploration of what drives markets and how it can be applied to client portfolios. Our culture of intellectual curiosity compels us to challenge the status quo, disrupt long-held beliefs and uncover new insights."

At the core of any enduring mission is intention. Not a casual intention, but one driven by deep emotional clarity. Unless that purpose carries a strong emotional charge, it will be difficult to sustain through volatility, rejection, and the inevitable cycles of doubt.

In their book *Choose Your Enemies Wisely*, Patrick Bet-David and Greg Dinkin argue that purpose sharpens not only when we know what we stand for, but also when we define what we stand against. By naming an "enemy", whether it is mediocrity, inefficiency, short-termism, or complacency, we create focus. Conflict, properly chosen, acts as a catalyst for energy and urgency.

For hedge fund leaders, this lesson is especially powerful. Investors are not only backing a stream of returns, but they are also backing the manager's resilience and the courage to stay the course when markets punish those who follow the herd. As Bet-David and Dinkin observe, history's most effective leaders-built loyalty by taking a stand against forces that weakened progress and clarity of purpose. The same is true in asset management. Allocators are drawn to managers whose brands are anchored in both conviction and emotional drive.

To create that kind of resonance, we must each discover the emotion that fuels us, the refusal to accept a certain outcome, the determination to solve a problem that others overlook, or the passion to protect what matters most. Intention without that emotional engine is hollow. Intention infused with it becomes a brand that feels inevitable, believable, and worth investing in.

Vision defines aspirations for the future. It defines leadership and reputational goals you aim to achieve. Typically, it emphasizes the role of collaboration, diversity, and continuous learning and considers aspects of client satisfaction, industry influence, and talent retention.

As an example, Henley Investment Management, an asset management firm focused on real estate, has a well-crafted vision statement: "To be trusted home for capital, known for smart investing." Some companies have a short statement like this one, while others go with one or more paragraphs to fully express themselves.

On the other hand, the set of values defines what is important to us and describes the ways we accomplish the stated mission. It defines guiding principles in our interaction with clients, stake-holders, and team members. It should reflect how excellence, innovation, and a client-centric approach shape your culture and delivery of your service.

Example of the Bridgewater Associates value statement: "Radical Truth and Transparency: At Bridgewater Associates, honesty and transparency are highly valued, with a culture that encourages open communication and constructive feedback.

Meritocracy: Bridgewater Associates is committed to a merit-based system that rewards employees based on their contributions and performance, rather than seniority or tenure. Meaningful Work and Meaningful Relationships: Bridgewater Associates believes that work should be fulfilling and meaningful, and that strong relationships with colleagues are essential to achieving this goal.

Responsibility: Bridgewater Associates emphasizes personal responsibility and accountability, with a culture that encourages employees to take ownership of their work and their impact on the organization."

Mission, value, and vision statements are not fixed in time. They do change. They can change as the circumstances around us change and as the company evolves. These statements not only define clear and coherent purpose, but they also serve as a foundation for decision making and strategic planning. They are there to inspire trust and loyalty and ultimately contribute to the sustained success of the firm.

Brand personality: Archetypes

Brands, like people, have their personalities. They carry attributes that describe their own level of openness, the way they communicate, their typical emotional dispositions, how they feel, and how they sound. The most successful brands in the world have well defined personalities, carefully crafted to facilitate connection and communication with their customers. To explore this further, let us go deeper into the field of psychology.

Swiss born Carl Gustav Jung (1875 to 1961) was a psychologist, psychotherapist, and a founder of the school of psychoanalysis. In the early stage of his career, he was a close friend of Sigmund Freud, with whom he shared a common vision of human psychology. Although complex and controversial during his lifetime, Jungwas one of the most influential psychologists in human history. He introduced the concepts of extraversion and introversion and established the theory of synchronicity, individuality, and the human unconscious.

In his work, Jung observed that all people, no matter where they live or which culture they belong to, share one universal conscious, a fundamental set of patterns of thoughts and behaviors. This conscious is fully embedded in all of us and represents all-inclusive impressions and experiences of our predecessors. He believed that the individual unconscious mind is influenced by the collective unconscious.

He explained that these impressions are expressed in various mythological and mystical characters and symbols that we know and associate with. Jung systemized them into twelve distinct groups called archetypes. For him, they represent basic human desires, such as the desire to seek adventure, express optimism, overcome obstacles, experience connection, and be wise.

Let's explore characteristics of the Jung's principal archetypes, how they translate to the hedge fund world, and how they are perceived by allocators.

The Innocent Archetype is characterized by eternal optimism, childlike wonder, and a lack of cynicism, as well as a yearning for simplicity. It aspires to a safer society and endeavors to improve it. It is distinguished by purity, vitality, optimism, morality, and kindness. Dove, Method, Volkswagen, and Ivory are among the brands that represent this concept.

A hedge fund that embodies the Innocent archetype presents itself as pure, transparent, and trustworthy, an antidote to the cynicism and opacity often associated with Wall Street. Its identity is built on simplicity and honesty, projecting an image of nothing to hide and a belief that investing should serve a greater good, not just financial gain. Instead of positioning markets as a battlefield or a puzzle, the Innocent views them as a landscape where careful stewardship, ethical choices, and long-term patience create genuine value.

The tone of communication is open, sincere, and optimistic, avoiding jargon in favor of clear and accessible language that makes investors feel safe and respected. Its visual identity leans toward light and fresh colors, white, soft blue, green, or gold, with clean design that emphasizes clarity and calmness.

Allocators interacting with an Innocent fund are meant to feel reassured that their capital is being handled with integrity and transparency, often reinforced by values driven investing, ESG integration, or socially conscious strategies.

Within the firm, the culture emphasizes ethics, humility, and a shared belief in doing the right thing for clients and society, creating an atmosphere of trust and loyalty. The strength of the Innocent lies in inspiring confidence through integrity and simplicity, but the challenge is to avoid appearing naive, overly idealistic, or lacking the competitive edge required in complex markets.

The Explorer Archetype is characterized by its innovative and ambitious nature, as it pushes boundaries in search of new frontiers. It aspires to perpetually preserve its autonomy.

Ambition, independence, individuality, and adventure comprise its strengths. NASA, Starbucks, Patagonia, and REI are among the brands that serve as examples.

A hedge fund that embodies the Explorer archetype positions itself as a bold seeker of new frontiers, constantly venturing into uncharted territories of the investment landscape to uncover hidden opportunities

Its identity is defined by curiosity, independence, and a restless drive to go where others will not, whether that means discovering overlooked small cap markets, pioneering new asset classes, or exploiting inefficiencies in emerging geographies.

The Explorer frames markets not as battlefields or puzzles, but as vast landscapes waiting to be charted, where value is revealed to those willing to journey beyond the obvious. Its tone of communication is adventurous yet disciplined, inspiring allocators with stories of discovery and differentiation, we look where others do not, we find what others miss.

The visual identity often leans on motifs of travel and discovery, compasses, maps, and horizons, paired with colors that suggest possibility and openness, such as deep teal, earthy greens, or sunrise golds. Allocators are meant to feel they are backing pioneers, managers with the courage and independence to differentiate from crowded consensus trades and deliver returns from unexplored niches.

Within the firm, culture thrives on curiosity, intellectual independence, and the freedom to think differently, rewarding those who challenge convention in pursuit of unique insights. The strength of the Explorer lies in its ability to stand apart, appealing to investors seeking true diversification, though its challenge is to avoid appearing unfocused, overly contrarian, or disconnected from practical constraints. In the hedge fund world, the Explorer archetype becomes a beacon for originality and courage, a firm that thrives on venturing beyond the well-worn path, discovering untapped opportunities, and inviting investors to join them on the journey of exploration

The Sage Archetype is a well of wisdom and intellect, offering guidance and advice. It desires to comprehend and establish clarity through analysis, comprehensive diligence, and reason. It is distinguished by its intelligence, insight, and knowledge. Wisdom, objectivity, credibility, and analytical rigor constitute its core strengths. Institutions and brands such as Harvard University, McKinsey & Company, The Economist, and Google exemplify the Sage archetype through their emphasis on knowledge, research, data-driven thinking, and authoritative guidance.

A hedge fund that embodies the Sage archetype positions itself as the voice of wisdom, insight, and intellectual rigor in an unpredictable financial world. Its identity is built on the promise of truth and understanding, emphasizing research depth, data driven analysis, and clarity of thought as the foundation for investment decisions. Rather than framing markets as battlefields, the Sage views them as puzzles to be solved, where patient inquiry and disciplined reasoning reveal enduring patterns and opportunities.

The tone of communication is thoughtful, authoritative, and measured, investor letters read more like essays or white papers, rich with context, historical perspective, and evidence.

Its visual identity often reflects restraint and clarity, using understated colors such as deep green, charcoal, or ivory, paired with simple and elegant typography to project trust and intellectual depth.

Allocators are meant to feel they are in the hands of seasoned advisors, partners who prioritize knowledge, transparency, and foresight over bravado.

Inside the firm, culture revolves around curiosity, collaboration, and a commitment to continuous learning, where every decision is informed by principles and tested against facts. The strength of the

Sage is in building long term credibility, earning loyalty through consistency and insight, though its challenge is avoiding paralysis from over analysis or appearing detached from the urgency of markets. In the hedge fund world, the Sage becomes a beacon of understanding, a trusted guide who distills complexity into clarity, transforming uncertainty into wisdom and knowledge into enduring value.

The Hero Archetype is a savior and redeemer who is characterized by courage, self-sacrifice, and achievement, and is a seeker of mastery. It is designed to facilitate personal growth and triumph over adversity. It was established with the intention of leaving a lasting impact and legacy. Inspiration, confidence, and honor comprise its strengths. Nike, Under Armour, and Doctors Without Borders are among the brands that serve as examples.

A hedge fund that embodies the Hero archetype presents itself as a disciplined, resilient, and courageous guardian of investor capital, defined by its ability to confront market volatility and emerge stronger. Its identity is built on the promise of strength in adversity, positioning markets as an arena of challenges to be conquered and inefficiencies as opportunities to be claimed. The Hero fund speaks in a direct and confident tone, framing its track record as proof of victory, navigating crises, protecting wealth, and delivering superior risk adjusted returns.

Its visual identity is bold and powerful, with strong colors like deep blue, black, and steel gray accented by red or gold, and symbols of strength, lions, shields, or mountains, that reinforce its determination and authority. Allocators are meant to feel that their capital is entrusted to a warrior like team, one that treats its mission with the discipline of elite athletes or soldiers and communicates results with clarity and pride. Yet the Hero archetype requires balance, while its narrative of triumph inspires trust and conviction, it must also temper confidence with humility to avoid arrogance and maintain credibility.

In the hedge fund world, the Hero firm becomes a beacon of reliability, a fighter for investor outcomes, and a symbol of excellence that inspires both allocators and employees to believe in its ability to withstand storms and seize victory.

The Rebel Archetype is characterized by a provocateur who endeavors to challenge the status quo by stretching the boundaries of convention. It strives for liberation and hopes to establish a legacy and impact. Rebelliousness and the capacity to drive change are its greatest assets. Harley Davidson, Virgin, and Levi Strauss and Co. are among the brands that serve as examples.

A hedge fund that embodies the Rebel archetype positions itself as a bold disruptor, unafraid to challenge conventions and break away from the traditional norms of asset management. Its identity is built on defiance, originality, and a refusal to accept the status quo, often framing mainstream strategies and consensus thinking as complacent or flawed. The Rebel fund thrives on contrarianism, finding alpha by going against the grain, taking bold stances, and uncovering value where others see only risk.

Its tone of communication is provocative, confident, and edgy, designed to capture attention and signal independence, we do not follow markets, we overturn them.

The visual identity often leans on stark, high contrast colors such as black, red, or metallics, paired with sharp and modern typography that conveys defiance and strength.

Allocators engaging with a Rebel fund are meant to feel they are partnering with a firm that will not hesitate to question authority, challenge orthodoxy, and take unconventional bets when the crowd is moving in the opposite direction.

Inside the organization, the culture prizes boldness, intellectual freedom, and individuality, empowering portfolio managers to speak their minds and pursue differentiated strategies.

The strength of the Rebel lies in its ability to attract investors who seek true differentiation and conviction, especially in times when conventional approaches underperform, though its challenge is to avoid recklessness or being perceived as overly combative.

In the hedge fund world, the Rebel archetype stands out as an unapologetic maverick, a firm that sees alpha not in following the rules but in rewriting them, inviting investors to join in reshaping the game itself.

The Magician Archetype possesses the capacity to comprehend hidden rules and to transform desires into tangible results. A trusted advisor and profound thinker, it aspires to authority and desires to leave a legacy. Vision, imagination, idealism, and charisma comprise its strengths. Disney, Polaroid, and Oculus are among the brands that serve as examples.

A hedge fund that embodies the Magician archetype positions itself as a transformative force, one that turns market complexity into opportunity with almost alchemical precision. Its identity is built on mastery, foresight, and the ability to see patterns invisible to others, creating the impression that it can bend volatility, uncertainty, and inefficiency into consistent returns. The Magician fund does not describe itself as merely reacting to markets, instead it projects the aura of foresight, using sophisticated models, deep research, and innovative strategies to anticipate shifts and unlock value.

Its tone of communication is visionary, confident, and inspiring, often blending technical depth with a sense of wonder, we make the unseen visible, we turn chaos into order.

The visual identity leans toward mystical or transformative imagery, light, prisms, geometric patterns, or cosmic themes, supported by colors like deep purple, midnight blue, silver, or gold that suggest mystery, mastery, and elegance.

Allocators are meant to feel they are partnering with a firm that has unique capabilities, one that can reveal hidden opportunities and deliver results in ways that seem almost beyond ordinary comprehension.

Internally, the culture thrives on innovation, intellectual curiosity, and cross disciplinary brilliance, attracting people who see finance not only as science but also as art.

The strength of the Magician lies in inspiring allocators with a sense of confidence and awe, positioning the firm as visionary and capable of transformation, though its challenge is to avoid appearing opaque or overly mysterious, which can trigger skepticism in a trust driven industry.

In the hedge fund world, the Magician archetype stands out as the transformer, turning insight into seemingly extraordinary outcomes.

The Citizen Archetype desires to be included and regards all individuals with the same respect. Its purpose is to act in a morally sound manner without seeking recognition. It is characterized by its efficacy, supportiveness, and strong character. AAA, Target, and The Home Depot are among the brands that serve as examples.

A hedge fund that embodies the Citizen archetype positions itself as grounded, approachable, and community minded, a firm that wins trust not by being flashy or combative but by being steady, relatable, and aligned with the values of its investors. Its identity is built on fairness, humility, and responsibility, projecting the idea that investing is not an elite game but a shared endeavor where everyone deserves transparency and respect. Unlike the Hero or Rebel, the Citizen fund does not claim to conquer or disrupt, instead it frames itself as a dependable partner, focused on long term stewardship and inclusive progress.

Its tone of communication is straightforward, honest, and down to earth, using plain language and emphasizing accessibility over jargon, we grow together, we rise together.

The visual identity often draws from approachable, human centric design, warm colors like green, blue, or soft earth tones, clean typography, and imagery that suggests cooperation, community, and trust.

Allocators are meant to feel that they are working with an ally who sees them not as transactions but as partners in a shared journey, often reinforced through ESG integration, responsible investing, or initiatives tied to societal contribution.

Internally, the culture values collaboration, respect, and equality, with a flat and team-oriented ethos rather than a hierarchical one.

The strength of the Citizen archetype lies in its ability to attract investors who value ethics, inclusivity, and long-term responsibility, though its challenge is to avoid being perceived as too ordinary, lacking the differentiation or edge that some allocators seek in hedge funds.

In the hedge fund world, the Citizen archetype stands out as the steady and principled steward, an honest and reliable firm that positions itself as part of the broader community, seeking not only returns but also to invest with integrity and responsibility.

The Lover Archetype is characterized by a desire to establish a connection with others and an admiration for beauty. It produces sensual and nurturing experiences that are both euphoric. It is distinguished by its vitality, appreciation, passion, and sensuality. Chanel, Tiffany and Co. and Haagen Dazs are among the brands that serve as examples.

A hedge fund that embodies the Lover archetype positions itself as deeply committed, passionate, and relationship driven, a firm that differentiates itself not through aggression or disruption but through the depth of connection it builds with its investors and the care it applies to capital stewardship. Its identity is rooted in intimacy, trust, and dedication, conveying the idea that investing is not just transactional but personal, requiring loyalty, devotion, and an alignment of values. Unlike the Hero who battles markets or the Explorer who chases new horizons, the Lover fund emphasizes closeness, understanding allocator needs, tailoring solutions, and creating a sense of partnership that transcends numbers.

Its tone of communication is warm, empathetic, and elegant, using language that reflects care and refinement, your capital is personal to us, we nurture it as we do our most important relationships.

The visual identity often leans on rich and sensual palettes, deep reds, burgundy, gold, or soft rose, paired with graceful typography and imagery evoking harmony, beauty, or human connection.

Allocators are meant to feel they are not just one client among many but a cherished partner whose trust is reciprocated with unwavering commitment.

Internally, the culture prioritizes loyalty, collaboration, and shared purpose, rewarding relationship building as highly as performance.

The strength of the Lover archetype lies in its ability to inspire trust through genuine intimacy and long-term dedication, appealing to investors who value partnership and emotional resonance; its challenge is to avoid appearing overly sentimental or lacking the toughness required in competitive markets.

In the hedge fund world, the Lover stands out as the devoted partner, an asset manager who not only delivers returns but also nurtures enduring bonds of trust and alignment with those who place capital in its care.

The Jester Archetype is characterized by a lighthearted, original narrator who mocks the conventional through humor or pointed satire. It seeks pleasure by establishing connections with others. It is distinguished by its humor, irreverence, and originality. Examples of brands include Ben and Jerry's, GEICO, and Jack in the Box.

A hedge fund that embodies the Jester archetype positions itself as playful, witty, and unconventional, using humor, creativity, and lightness to disarm the formality and rigidity of the investment world. Its identity is rooted in the belief that finance does not always need to be dour or intimidating, and that fresh perspectives often emerge when people are free to laugh, question, and think differently. Unlike the Sage who emphasizes wisdom or the Hero who stresses discipline, the Jester fund thrives on breaking tension, cutting through jargon, and making complexity approachable with levity and clever insights.

Its tone of communication is lively, irreverent, and engaging, using sharp humor, memorable metaphors, or unexpected storytelling to stand out, "Markets are serious enough, we prefer to find opportunity where others only see drama."

The visual identity leans toward vibrant colors like orange, yellow, turquoise, or bright contrasts, paired with playful and bold typography and imagery that suggests creativity, spontaneity, or joy.

Allocators interacting with a Jester-style fund feel they are working with a team unafraid to challenge conventions, bringing lightness to heavy conversations while still delivering sharp and insightful perspectives.

Internally, the culture values humor, creativity, and camaraderie, encouraging people to take their work seriously but not themselves, fostering innovation by keeping minds open and stress low. The strength of the Jester archetype lies in its ability to differentiate, humanize, and build strong rapport with allocators, particularly those tired of generic and overly formal presentations; its challenge is to balance humor with credibility so as not to appear flippant or unserious in a trust-based industry.

In the hedge fund world, the Jester stands out as the refreshing contrarian, a firm that injects wit and humanity into finance, reminding investors that the best ideas often come from those who dare to play while others are paralyzed by fear.

The Guardian Archetype selflessly provides care and nurtures others. It is of the opinion that its duty is to help and establish stability. Its fundamental aspiration is to render assistance to others. CVS, Johnson and Johnson, and UNICEF are among the brands that serve as examples.

A hedge fund that embodies the Guardian archetype positions itself as the steadfast protector of investor capital, an institution defined by safety, stability, and prudence above all else. Its identity is rooted in trust, responsibility, and vigilance, presenting the firm as a careful steward whose primary mission is preservation before growth. Unlike the Hero who seeks victory or the Rebel who thrives on disruption, the Guardian fund emphasizes security, minimizing downside risk, safeguarding wealth through market turbulence, and ensuring clients can sleep at night knowing their capital is in safe hands.

Its tone of communication is calm, reassuring, and measured, highlighting reliability and discipline, "Our role is to protect what you have built, so it endures across generations."

The visual identity often draws on symbols of strength and permanence, fortresses, shields, or oak trees, paired with muted and stable colors like navy, gray, forest green, or bronze that signal safety and tradition.

Allocators interacting with a Guardian-style fund are meant to feel reassured, perceiving the firm as a safe harbor in stormy seas, which is particularly attractive for pensions, endowments, or family offices with an emphasis on intergenerational wealth.

Internally, the culture prizes caution, responsibility, and long-term orientation, rewarding measured decision-making and collective accountability rather than reckless risk-taking.

The strength of the Guardian archetype lies in its ability to build enduring trust and loyalty, positioning the firm as a bulwark against uncertainty, though its challenge is to avoid appearing overly conservative, slow-moving, or unimaginative in dynamic markets. In the hedge fund world, the Guardian stands out as the vigilant steward, a protector of capital who ensures that wealth is not only grown but safeguarded, honoring the ultimate duty of care to investors.

The Artist Archetype is characterized by a fervor for self-expression and innovation. It provides innovative solutions and addresses the requirements of individuals. Providing structure and innovation are its objectives. Creativity, entrepreneurship, and imagination comprise its strengths. Apple, Adobe, and LEGO are among the brands that serve as examples.

A hedge fund that embodies the Artist archetype positions itself as a creator of beauty, elegance, and originality within the financial markets, treating investment management not merely as science or competition, but as a refined craft. Its identity is rooted in creativity, imagination, and the pursuit of harmony, projecting the sense that portfolios are not just constructed but composed, with the care and intentionality of a masterpiece.

Unlike the Sage who focuses on knowledge or the Hero who focuses on conquest, the Artist fund emphasizes vision and expression, seeing markets as a canvas where patterns, themes, and stories can be woven into strategies that are as inspiring as they are profitable. Its tone of communication is refined, graceful, and metaphorical, often describing investment processes in terms of design, balance, and long-term artistry, "We do not just build portfolios, we craft them with intention."

The visual identity draws on aesthetics associated with elegance and creativity, flowing lines, abstract patterns, or minimalist forms, paired with palettes of deep jewel tones, muted golds, or soft pastels that suggest sophistication and taste.

Allocators engaging with an Artist-style fund are meant to feel they are partnering with a firm that offers not just returns but an elevated experience, where clarity, originality, and a sense of refinement set it apart from more mechanical competitors.

Inside the firm, the culture thrives on inspiration, originality, and a passion for craft, encouraging employees to think differently, honor nuance, and refine strategies with the precision of artisans.

The strength of the Artist archetype lies in differentiation and emotional resonance, appealing to investors who value originality and sophistication, though its challenge is to avoid being seen as impractical or too abstract in a results-driven industry.

In the hedge fund world, the Artist stands out as the visionary craftsman, a manager who elevates investing into an art form, blending creativity and precision to create strategies that endure with both beauty and impact.

The Ruler Archetype is a leader of the group who is confident, commanding, and potent. It aspires to establish control and structure. It demonstrates strengths in the areas of leadership, organization, and responsibility. The brands like Rolex, Rolls Royce, and Lloyds are among the Ruler archetypes. A hedge fund that embodies the Ruler archetype positions itself as authoritative, commanding, and built for long-term dominance, an institution that inspires confidence through order, discipline, and control.

Its identity is rooted in stability, structure, and mastery, projecting the image of a firm that not only manages capital but gov erns it with absolute rigor. Unlike the Hero who thrives on courage or the Explorer who thrives on discovery, the Ruler fund emphasizes leadership and reliability, setting the rules of the game rather than merely playing it.

Its tone of communication is formal, deliberate, and commanding, underscoring its ability to impose structure and discipline on the chaos of markets, "We create order where others see uncertainty, we lead so your capital endures."

The visual identity leans toward regal and authoritative symbolism, crowns, pillars, eagles, or geometric precision, paired with stately colors such as deep navy, royal blue, black, or gold that signal power and permanence.

Allocators are meant to feel that they are entrusting their capital to a sovereign institution, one that has the authority, systems, and discipline to protect wealth and expand it across generations.

Internally, the culture prizes excellence, accountability, and hierarchy, rewarding performance and reinforcing a sense of belonging to an elite institution that demands the best.

The strength of the Ruler archetype lies in its ability to project gravitas and stability, attracting investors who value safety, structure, and enduring influence, though its challenge is to avoid appearing rigid, overly conservative, or disconnected from innovation.

In the hedge fund world, the Ruler stands out as the commanding leader, a firm that offers allocators not just returns but the assurance of authority, order, and disciplined stewardship in an uncertain financial landscape.

Application to the branding

In 2001, Margaret Mark and Carol Pearson published "The Hero and the Outlaw" where they introduced Jung's archetype concept to the science of branding to help brands create deeper connections with their audiences. They provided a matrix of various personalities that can apply to the branding of services and products.

Behind any action there is a motivation. Motivation is the reason why an audience connects to the brand. There are certain needs that they believe will be fulfilled by using the product or service of that particular brand. Maslow identified these as basic needs, the need to exist, the need for safety and stability, and the need for change and surprise. Then there is the need to relate, the need to have importance and meaning, to be wanted, and to have connection with others. Finally, there is the need to grow through personal development or through contribution to serve and help.

Following Maslow's research, Adler expanded the findings and concluded that these needs are intertwined simultaneously and are not satisfied in hierarchy. He found that our motivations are expressed by various combinations of these basic needs and various levels of their intensities.

The archetypes call upon these basic needs and create a bridge between our product or service and the client's desire for meaning. The archetypes act as triggers to establish an emotional attachment to the brand. It may be sufficient to just mention small clues associated with a specific archetype for the subconscious mind to put together the rest of the brand narrative.

As brand relationships with audiences became more complex over time, brand personalities evolved and became more complex as well. The study of the Kelley School of Business at Indiana University in 2022, in their survey of 2400 brands, showed that strong and successful brands tend to portray multiple archetypes rather than just one as previously believed.

Nowadays, they argue, customers want brands that have nothing to hide and that express their views in many different aspects of life. Modern brands tend to have more frequent interactions with their audience, and they communicate through diverse channels. Due to digital media and technology, brands are becoming democratized, and social media allows audiences to take over the brand narrative.

That is how the archetype matrix gets redefined. The archetypes can be grouped based on the core basic need they fulfill:

Need to Exist: Sage, Magician, Explorer, and Jester

Need to Relate: Ruler, Rebel, Hero, and Lover

Need to Grow: Citizen, Innocent, Artist, and Guardian

At the same time, each of the archetypes has a subcategory further fine-tuning the exact emotional experience they fulfill.

While communicating the brand story, the primary and secondary archetypes are not introduced all at once. Successful brands introduce archetypes in layers through various touchpoints in the customer journey.

The goal in brand creation is to find the most suitable archetype which will best describe corporate culture, its people, mission, vision, and values. Once the archetypes have been selected, they have to become a part of all aspects of brand expression. They are meant to transpire through all presentations, communications, interactions, visual identity, and ultimately brand experience.

As it applies to the hedge fund industry, different archetypes are used depending on the strategy and the style. The most common ones are the Sage, the Explorer, the Hero, the Ruler, and the Guardian.

Here are a few AI-generated examples of how well-known hedge fund brands apply archetypes in their branding. Point72, founded by Steve Cohen, can be associated with the Explorer archetype in terms of branding. The Explorer archetype is characterized by a desire for discovery, innovation, and pushing boundaries. Point72 is known for its dynamic and entrepreneurial approach to investing, constantly seeking new opportunities and strategies to generate returns. The firm emphasizes a culture of learning, adaptability, and exploration, encouraging its team to think creatively and pursue new frontiers in the investment landscape. This aligns with the Explorer's spirit of adventure and curiosity in the financial world.

Millennium Management can be associated with the "Sage" archetype in terms of branding. This archetype is characterized by careful planning, adaptability, and a focus on achieving long-term goals. Millennium Management is known for its multi-strategy approach, employing a diverse range of investment strategies to navigate complex markets. The firm emphasizes risk management, innovation, and a collaborative environment, projecting an image of being a calculated and forward-thinking player in the hedge fund industry.

Citadel, founded by Ken Griffin, can be associated with the "Ruler" archetype in terms of branding. The Ruler archetype is about control, authority, and creating order out of chaos.

Citadel is known for its strong leadership, disciplined approach to investing, and cutting-edge technology, which allows it to maintain a dominant position in the financial markets. The firm projects an image of power, precision, and excellence, striving to be a leader in the hedge fund industry.

Bridgewater Associates can be seen as embodying the "Sage" archetype. The Sage archetype is characterized by a commitment to knowledge, truth, and understanding.

Bridgewater's emphasis on data-driven decision-making, extensive research, and a culture of radical transparency aligns well with the qualities of the Sage. The firm positions itself as a thought leader in the financial industry, offering insights and expertise on complex economic issues.

Renaissance Technologies can be associated with the "Magician" archetype in terms of branding. The Magician archetype is characterized by transformation, innovation, and the ability to see beyond the ordinary. Renaissance Technologies is renowned for its pioneering use of quantitative analysis and sophisticated algorithms to drive investment decisions. The firm is often seen as mysterious and highly innovative, leveraging advanced mathematics and data science to achieve remarkable returns. This aligns with the Magician's image of using knowledge and technology to create seemingly magical outcomes in the financial world.

Tonality

Tonality defines how a brand speaks to its audience. It defines how the audience hears the message. The tonality of the brand has the ability to evoke certain emotions in the audience.

Depending on how the brand wants to be perceived, it might choose a formal authoritative voice or choose to sound casual and informal and inspire trust, comfort, or nostalgia. The emotional connection with the audience will strengthen brand loyalty and engagement. Tonality can be an effective differentiator from competitors and can leave a memorable imprint in the mind of the audience.

The tonality of the brand should match the selected archetype of the brand. It should be aligned with the brand's North Star statements, mission, vision, and values. The consistent tone across all communication channels, whether emails, presentations, videos, live meetings, or even music on hold, reinforces the brand's identity and ensures that the brand is easily recognizable. All the members of the organization, not just client facing teams, should be aware of and adopt and implement the tonality and voice of the brand.

Brand Visual Identity

Logo

Design of the logo seeks to integrate the meaning of the brand and its form. It puts together the entire complexity of the brand into one visual symbol, whose look and feel becomes immediately recognizable. Design of the logo has to incorporate the brand personality and serve as its extension and form of expression.

As Louise Fili, award winning New York based graphic design expert once said, "A logo is a typographic portrait, the face of the business. I talk to clients at length, learning everything about them, who they are, what is important to them, and then translate it. A great logo appears effortless and is, of course, anything but."

Typography

Typography is another branding element that plays a crucial role in shaping a brand's identity. Like logo and colors, it serves as a visual and communicative tool that affects how the brand is perceived by its audience. The choice of fonts can convey a wide range of emotions and attributes such as sophistication, playfulness, reliability, or modernity. For instance, a luxury brand might opt for a serif font to evoke elegance and tradition, while a tech startup might use a sleek sans serif font to suggest innovation and simplicity.

Typography encapsulates the brand's personality and helps communicate its message more effectively. The right typography can enhance readability, create a visual hierarchy, and guide the audience's attention to key messages. Moreover, consistent typography use helps build brand recognition as consumers associate specific font styles with the brand. When typography aligns with the brand's values and personality, it strengthens the overall brand identity and creates a cohesive visual experience.

Colors

Colors influence emotions. Many healing therapies use different sections of the color spectrum to evoke positive, uplifting, or calming emotions. Brands can use their colors to match the personality of the brand and fortify its communication with the target audience. Some well-known brands, like Tiffany and Co, are distinctly recognizable by their brand color.

Brand colors should be distinctive compared to competitors. They should have a positive connotation to the target market and be culturally accepted in the parts of the world where the brand operates. Brand colors should be in coherence with selected brand archetypes. The brands in the financial industry have been using colors of blue, gray, green, white, and black as their colors of preference. These colors indicate confidence, dependability, wealth, prosperity, authority, and craftsmanship. While keeping these colors as primary, there has been more experimentation with the choices for accent colors, where we see use of orange, purple, magenta, and gold.

It is important to understand practical considerations when choosing the color palettes. Can we achieve consistency across different media and across devices. How does the color present itself when used in large scale. Does the color have a positive connotation for the target market and is it culturally accepted in other parts of the world.

Tagline

It is interesting to mention that we do not see the use of taglines in the hedge fund industry. Several reasons contribute to that. The target audience of hedge funds are sophisticated institutional investors or high net worth individuals who do not respond to a tagline as a broad audience would. There is a high level of exclusivity and prestige that hedge funds maintain.

Historically, they tend to maintain a low profile and typically rely on word of mouth and reputation rather than broader marketing.

Hedge funds provide a complex set of services and nuances of products, making it challenging to encapsulate them in a single tagline. The financial industry, including hedge funds, is heavily regulated which can limit the use of promotional language like taglines. In recent years, we have seen democratization in alternative investments, hedge funds included, which is slowly but surely broadening their target audience, causing branding methods to evolve. As the regulatory framework changes and allows firms to market to a broader audience, we might see more use of taglines in the future.

According to brand experts Wheeler and Mayer (2016), the tagline should be short and unique, it should capture the brand's essence and positioning, and it should be easy to say and remember. Taglines, like colors, can evoke emotional responses and have the ability to connect with the audience on a deeper level.

When crafted effectively, a tagline expresses the unsolved desire of the target audience. It taps into deep seated needs, aspirations, and emotions that the audience might not even fully articulate themselves. By resonating with these latent desires, the brand can establish an immediate connection with the audience and position itself as a solution to unmet needs.

Taglines can be descriptive and describe the service and brand promise. For example, "Expect more, pay less" (Target), "Building a better working world" (Ernst and Young), and "The quicker picker upper" (Bounty). They can also express the brand in superlative form and present the company as best in class. For example, "Diamonds are forever" (De Beers), "The ultimate driving machine" (BMW), and "Impossible is nothing" (Adidas). They can be provocative and thought provoking. For example, "Can you hear me now" (Verizon Wireless), "Got milk" (Dairy Management), and "What is in your wallet" (Capital One Bank).

Taglines can also reveal the business category. For example, "Drivers wanted" (Volkswagen), "Love the skin you are in" (Olay), and "Happy hunting" (eBay). Taglines can also command action and be imperative. Examples are "Feel the love" (Crocs), "Belong anywhere" (Airbnb), and "Think different" (Apple).

When crafting a tagline for a hedge fund, it is important to convey reliability, trust, expertise, and the unique value your fund offers. Client centric approach, innovation driven growth, and long-term vision are a few fund characteristics that can drive the creation of the tagline.

Brand Communication

The benefits of all market research and analysis done to set up the brand so far cannot be fully utilized if we fail to communicate properly.

When we look at the parties involved with the fund, both internally and externally, there are several circles of communication that stand out. These include internal communication, which involves all employees and third-party service providers, communication with investors, including current limited partners, and communication with the public, which includes prospective investors and the general audience.

It is essential that all stakeholders receive the same message. Information should be released from one centralized source. The timing and order of the release are also critical. The employees and partners of the firm should know information before it is made public.

Very often, when markets go through adversity and performance is affected, many funds tend to pull back and decide not to communicate until they remedy the situation and regain performance. However, the practice should be the opposite. Reaching out proactively to investors and other related parties is the best course of action. Sharing concerns and expressing humility rein-forces relationships and builds trust.

Touchpoints in the prospect's journey

When it comes to approaching new investors, communication should be skillfully crafted. In the last decade, the process of engaging and winning new investors has become significantly longer and more complex. Getting to know someone takes time; it is a process. Each time we connect or meet, more information is revealed, and the picture of the other party or person becomes more complete.

New prospects embark on a journey from the first day they learn about the fund up to the moment they commit to allocate and even beyond. Each time, a prospect gains a little more in-depth information about the strategy and the firm.

Many times, we see hedge fund introductions sharing too much too soon, practically overwhelming the prospective investor and losing them at the very beginning of the relationship.

It the process of buying product or service, there are four physiological stages that a buyer typically goes through. These are **Awareness, Consideration, Interest, and Engagement.**

Awareness – In this stage, prospects come across the fund strategy for the first time. They may have learned about the strategy through a database, a conference, or your first outreach. Messaging in this stage should be clear and concise, not overly detailed, yet captivating enough to attract the prospect's attention.

Consideration – When investors request an in person meeting or an introductory conference call, they are in the stage where they are interested in learning more about the fund. Messaging in this stage should provide evidence to support the claims the brand makes.

Interest – Follow-up communication after initial meetings is where you learn more about the prospective investor.

Typically, messaging in this stage focuses on what the prospect wants but has not yet been able to achieve, and how the brand can help. It appeals to desire. Messaging should create a sense of tension and polarity, helping the prospect envision transformation through the fund's value proposition.

Engagement– In this stage, the brand communicates how easy and simple it is to do business with them. Messaging provides a clear and straightforward pathway to the next step. Typically, the prospect

reaches this stage after several due diligence meetings and is close to making a decision.

Each of these stages requires different messaging, each adding unique value to the target audience. The messaging must provide relevant information, add value, and create an emotional impact that influences the decision-making process of the prospect.

These stages often blend into one another. It is both an art and a science to recognize them and adjust the messaging accordingly. As mentioned earlier, the process of fundraising is not linear, and the stages of the journey do not last the same amount of time for each prospect. They are unique for every individual, and messaging must be tailored to each relationship, especially in the later stages of interaction.

The goal here is to become well-versed in recognizing what type of messaging to apply based on the particular conversation with the prospect. The skill of listening with attention and intention to learn about the prospect comes to the forefront.

Storytelling

"The most powerful person in the world is the storyteller."
Steve Jobs, quoted in James Webb's The Guts to Try (1992)

Storytelling has been part of human history for thousands of years. Stories are how humans' bond, relate, and share experiences. They hold significant influence over our emotional and psychological states.

According to Hasson (2016), a psychology and neuroscience professor at Princeton University, the brainwaves of the storyteller and the listeners start to synchronize as the story unfolds. The better the audience comprehends the story, and the more common understanding they share, the more their brainwaves mirror each other. The expression "we are on the same wavelength" most likely originates from this concept.

What Kind of Stories Can You Tell?

When it comes to storytelling, the possibilities are vast. Creating narratives around founders, partners, employees, or others involved in building the fund can showcase significant impact. Sharing the story of how you discovered the alpha of your strategy, or including powerful anecdotes and constructive feedback from investors, can add depth and credibility to your brand narrative.

Stories must be relevant and told for a clear reason. Each story should connect to topics that matter to investors and align with the differentiators they care about. Stories tied to any of the previously mentioned diversifiers make excellent foundations for impactful narratives.

People are drawn to personal stories. Articulating your great-est motivations and revealing the driving forces behind your efforts gives investors deeper insight into your conviction and what compels you to seize opportunities others might overlook. The most impactful stories resonate with the human experience, so include personal narratives that connect on an emotional level.

If you aim to highlight specific qualities, emphasize reliability, transparency, and honesty, enabling investors to trust in your commitments. The more authentic your story is, the more deeply it will resonate with your audience.

Finally, sharing valuable lessons and challenges you have encountered and overcome while investing, trading, or managing your business can be both captivating and inspiring to investors. These reflections demonstrate resilience and the ability to learn and adapt, qualities that enhance your brand's credibility.

Three Core Elements of Effective Storytelling

Capturing Attention

Stories must quickly capture attention, especially in today's digital age of distractions. Utilizing a hook, suspense, or an unexpected twist at the beginning can pique interest and stimulate dopamine, a neurotransmitter linked to focus and attention. Additionally, visually engaging content such as videos or infographics can effectively grab attention because the brain processes images rapidly.

Creating Emotional Connection

Emotional connections are the bedrock of powerful storytelling, forging a bond between the narrative and the audience. Stories that stir emotions like joy, sadness, hope, or fear have the potential to inspire action and foster deeper connections. When char-acters and scenarios mirror the audience's values and experiences, they create empathy and emotional investment. Neuroscience re-search indicates that stories can trigger the release of hormones like oxytocin, which is associated with trust and empathy, further strengthening this emotional bond.

Transforming Perspective

Stories have the power to influence beliefs, shift attitudes, and in-spire behavioral change by fostering a sense of shared experience. This phenomenon, known as narrative transportation, occurs when the audience becomes deeply immersed in the story, significantly affecting their attitudes and behaviors. Well-crafted narratives can challenge existing assumptions, introduce new perspectives, and empower individuals to overcome personal challenges, resulting in transformation and growth.

Structured stories play a crucial role in helping audiences grasp and retain complex information, leading to new insights and knowledge. By effectively incorporating all three elements, a story evolves from a mere sequence of events into a compelling experience that resonates with the audience, influencing their thoughts, feelings, and actions long after engagement.

How to Structure the Story

We can tell stories in our own unique way as long as we remain authentic and emotionally honest. However, structure provides the story with the dynamics necessary to create a bond between the narrator and the audience.

Below are a few storytelling frameworks that can be particularly effective when crafting your brand story:

1. The Classic Narrative Structure Character → Conflict → Resolution

This three-act structure is one of the most natural storytelling formats and adapts seamlessly to hedge fund narratives.

Act I: Character

In Act I, the "character" is introduced, the fund, its founder, or its core strategy. This establishes the foundation by clarifying what drives the manager and what problem they set out to solve. By humanizing the fund as a character, the story becomes accessible and memorable, allowing readers to engage with it as they would with a protagonist in a novel.

Act II: Conflict

Act II introduces conflict, the essential ingredient for drama and tension. Hedge funds rarely succeed without adversity, and this is where the true test unfolds. Market turbulence, regulatory pressures, operational hurdles, and investor skepticism all serve as obstacles. Sharing these challenges not only heightens engagement but also builds credibility by showing that success did not come easily.

Act III: Resolution

Resolution arrives in Act III. Here, the manager demonstrates how challenges were overcome through discipline, innovation, or perseverance. The payoff is more than just performance; it is a transformation. The narrative closes with insights that readers can apply, reinforcing the idea that resilience, adaptability, and clarity of vision are central to success.

From the allocator's perspective, this structure resonates because it mirrors their own due diligence journey: act I answer questions about identity and motivation; act II reassures them that the manager has been tested by real-world challenges and act III provides evidence of adaptability and offers a clear rationale for investment.

For allocators, the three-act structure delivers both the emotional engagement of a story and the rational confidence needed to justify an allocation decision.

Example: Renaissance Technologies and the Medallion Fund

Act I – Character: Renaissance Technologies began as Jim Simons's attempt to turn mathematics into a trading edge.

Simons, a former academic and codebreaker, founded the firm that became Renaissance in 1978 and deliberately filled it with scientists and mathematicians, people like Leonard Baum and James Ax, rather than traditional Wall Street stock-pickers.

That talent base produced the Medallion Fund, launched in 1988 as Renaissance's proprietary, model-driven strategy (Wikipedia, 2024; Wikipedia, 2024).

Act II – Conflict: The early Medallion Fund struggled. By April 1989 it had fallen roughly 30% from peak, triggering internal debate about whether the models were viable in live markets. James Ax wanted to push ahead. Simons wanted to pause and rethink. The tension nearly split the project and forced a redesign of both process and leadership (Wikipedia, 2024).

Act III – Resolution: Simons brought in Elwyn Berlekamp to rebuild the system and refine execution. Within a year the fund's performance turned sharply upward. What followed became industry legend: over the next three decades, Medallion generated on the order of 66% average annual returns before fees and about 39% after fees from 1988 through 2018, an outcome that produced more than $100 billion in gains and established Renaissance as the most successful quantitative trading firm in history (Quantified Strategies, 2025; Pyrford, 2024; Wikipedia, 2024).

Allocator's Perspective: Allocators see a narrative of a visionary founder, Simons, tested by early volatility, who responded with expertise, collaboration, and innovation, ultimately delivering consistent, industry-leading performance. The story portrays an investment opportunity that feels both bold and defensible.

2. The Hero's Journey Structure

While the **Classic Narrative Structure** tells a clear story of challenge and resolution, showing how a fund was built or recovered from setbacks, the **Hero's Journey** goes deeper. It focuses on transformation, not just results. The manager steps into uncertainty, faces market trials, learns hard lessons, and returns with greater insight and discipline. This approach highlights evolution and resilience rather than performance alone. In short, it's not only about how the fund performed, but how the manager grew through the experience.

The Hero's Journey provides a dramatic, almost mythic frame-work for telling hedge fund stories. It begins with the call to adventure: a manager recognizes a market inefficiency or envisions a bold strategy. This moment establishes the fund's purpose and vision, and it makes the manager's decision to step away from convention, feel courageous and visionary.

The narrative then moves into trials and allies, where the manager encounters obstacles. Raising capital amid skepticism, building infrastructure, and weathering early setbacks all form part of this stage. Yet along the way, allies emerge: an anchor investor, a loyal team, or a mentor. These figures bring credibility and social proof to the story, showing that others believed in the mission when few did.

The abyss and transformation are central to the arc. A near-failure or crisis tests the fund's very existence, yet from this crucible emerges resilience and clarity. The return with the elixir demonstrates that the fund has been tested, refined, and is now ready to deliver durable results. For readers, this arc feels epic, elevating the hedge fund experience into a story of vision, struggle, and ultimate triumph.

For allocators, the Hero's Journey appeals to both emotion and logic. They see managers who have been tested in fire and emerged stronger. They relate to the skepticism, since they often voice it themselves, and they find comfort in the allies who validate the journey. Most importantly, they value the "elixir," the proven, resilient strategy that emerges after transformation. This structure convinces them not just of potential, but of durability.

Example: Ray Dalio and Bridgewater Associates

Call to Adventure: Ray Dalio founded Bridgewater Associates in 1975, operating out of his two-bedroom Manhattan apartment after being fired from a Wall Street job. His ambition was to build an investment firm grounded on systematic analysis rather than conventional intuition (Investopedia, 2022; Bridgewater, n.d.).

Trials & Allies: Over the early years, Dalio navigated the challenge of winning institutional clients—among them McDonald's and the World Bank pension fund—and steadily built the firm through rigorous research and a principles-driven culture. Bridgewater's early growth was anchored in its subscription research business and advisory work before evolving into full asset-management (Wikipedia, 2024; Bridgewater, n.d.).

Abyss and Transformation: The 2008 global financial crisis tested Bridgewater's macro-investment approach. Dalio's culture of radical transparency and systematic decision-making, what he calls an idea meritocracy, was credited with helping the firm navigate the turbulence and emerge as a leader in hedge-fund investing (Investopedia, 2022; New Yorker, 2011).

Return with the Elixir: Dalio published his management and investment philosophy in *Principles*, thereby sharing his ethos of openness, systemization and learning. Under his leadership Bridgewater grew to become one of the largest hedge-fund firms in the world, offering allocators a model of institutional scale, disciplined process and cultural coherence (Bridgewater, n.d.; Wikipedia, 2024).

Allocator's Perspective: Allocators resonate with Dalio's journey because it combines vision with challenge, systematic culture with performance, and endures as a replicable investment philosophy, giving them both narrative and operational confidence.

3. The Problem–Solution–Impact Structure

The Problem–Solution–Impact framework is clear, rational, and highly aligned with allocator psychology. It begins with the problem, which defines the gap in the market or the unmet investor need. This stage grabs attention immediately because it speaks to what allocators are already thinking: where are my blind spots, and who can help me solve them?

The second stage presents the solution: the strategy, culture, or structure the fund has designed to address the problem. This is where differentiation is highlighted. The fund demonstrates how it has engineered a repeatable process, crafted a unique edge, or solved something that competitors have ignored.

Allocators value this clarity because it helps them place the fund within their broader portfolio context.

Finally, the story emphasizes impact. Results in terms of returns are important, but allocators also look for resilience under stress and long-term value creation. By showcasing tangible outcomes, whether in performance, risk management, or branding strength, the fund ties the narrative back to investor goals. This structure works especially well for complex strategies as it simplifies them into a clear "problem–solution–result" flow.

From the allocator's perspective, this framework reduces friction in the decision-making process. It reassures them that the fund understands their pain points, offers a tailored solution, and can demonstrate tangible impact. In a world where allocators hear hundreds of pitches, this clarity sets the fund apart, making it easier to evaluate, remember, and justify to an investment committee.

Example: Renaissance Technologies

Problem: Many investors sought robust alpha, only to find that human-driven strategies often proved inconsistent, opaque or too expensive.

Solution: Renaissance Technologies developed a data-driven model-based trading approach. Its flagship fund, the Medallion Fund, operates via scalable quantitative systems and scientific talent, deploying mathematical models and automated trading to target persistent market inefficiencies (Wikipedia, 2024; Quantified Strategies, 2024).

Impact: The Medallion Fund delivered extraordinary results: over three decades it achieved an average annualized net return of around 39% after fees, and approximately 66% before fees, from 1988 onwards, generating more than US$100 billion in trading profits and cementing the brand as synonymous with state-of-the-art quantitative investing (Quantified Strategies, 2024; Institutional Investor, 2021).

Allocator's Perspective: Allocators see a clear narrative, a market problem addressed via a scientifically rigorous solution that resulted in extraordinary outcomes. The structure provides clarity, differentiation, and justification for allocation.

4. The Tension & Release Structure

The tension and release method thrives on drama. The narrative begins by setting the stage with a vivid market backdrop: perhaps the exuberance of the dot-com boom, the collapse of the global financial crisis, or the uncertainty of the COVID crash. This instantly grounds the reader in a recognizable moment of risk and opportunity.

Tension builds when the fund takes a contrarian or bold stance. Going against consensus, doubling down when others retreat, or positioning for a dramatic event creates suspense. Listeners lean in because they want to know whether the decision pays off or collapses. The heightened sense of risk makes the unfolding outcome all the more gripping.

The release delivers resolution, whether in the form of a spectacular win, a painful loss, or a strategic reinvention.

Reflection then ties the experience back to brand identity: was the fund vindicated as visionary, or was it reshaped through humility and adaptation? Either way, the story creates a memorable turning point that defines how the fund is perceived.

For allocators, this structure resonates because it mirrors their own lived experiences. They too feel the tension of market cycles and crave the release of clarity. Watching how a manager navigates this arc reassures them of the fund's ability to handle volatility, conviction, and pressure. It offers insight into character as much as strategy, and it leaves allocators with a vivid story to retell internally when championing the fund.

Example: Bridgewater's Risk Parity All Weather and Pure Alpha Strategies

Set the Stage: In the early 1990s, market turmoil and uncertainty demanded more resilient strategies. Many institutional allocators feared systemic collapses and sought portfolios built for multiple economic regimes (Bridgewater Associates, n.d.; MarketsWiki, 2023).

Tension Builds: Bridgewater launched its flagship Pure Alpha fund in 1989 and followed with the All-Weather strategy in 1996, embracing global-macro diversification and risk-parity techniques at a time when most peers remained heavily equity-biased (MarketsWiki, 2023; S&P / SPDJI, 2022).

Release: Pure Alpha demonstrated portfolios with only rare down years, benefiting from Bridgewater's systematic approach during crises. Meanwhile, All Weather became a go-to strategy for many institutions seeking stable, long-term growth irrespective of market direction (Bridgewater Associates, n.d.; S&P / SPDJI, 2022).

Reflection: These strategies cemented Bridgewater's reputation for innovative risk management and strategic foresight, turning volatility into opportunity and helping the firm become one of the largest hedge fund operators globally (MarketsWiki, 2023).

Allocator's Perspective: Allocators connect with this drama: tension in markets, confident contrarian positioning, and clarity of outcome. The story reassures them that the manager can with-stand uncertainty and deliver consistent outcomes when many cannot.

5. Story of Brand Archetype Structure

The archetype lens reframes hedge funds not as abstract entities but as living brands with symbolic identities. By defining a fund as a Hero, Sage, Explorer, or Rebel, the narrative communicates personality and purpose instantly. This simplifies perception for listeners, who can quickly grasp what the fund represents without wading through technical details.

The second stage brings these traits to life. A Hero fund demonstrates relentless drive for performance, a Sage embodies wisdom and analysis, an Explorer thrives on venturing into frontier markets, and a Rebel challenges convention with bold moves. By grounding strategy in culture, the fund creates an identity that feels coherent and memorable.

Conflict adds depth, since every archetype carries weaknesses. Heroes risk overreach, Sages may appear detached, Explorers face skepticism, and Rebels risk alienation. The resolution shows how the fund adapts, survives, or evolves, reinforcing its ability to endure. This cycle of archetype, challenge, and evolution creates both drama and brand resilience.

Allocators respond strongly to archetypes because they simplify complexity. When reviewing dozens of managers, archetypes serve as shorthand for identity and behavior. They help allocators remember not just what a fund does, but who it is. A Rebel fund might be risky, but it stands out. A Sage fund might feel safer, but it reassures with intellectual credibility.

By framing identity in archetypal terms, managers give allocators the language to retell the story persuasively to colleagues and investment committees.

Example: AQR Capital Management as "The Sage and Educator"

Introduce Archetype: AQR Capital Management embodies the Sage archetype with a pronounced Educator edge. It's very name, Applied Quantitative Research signals the brand promise: insight grounded in evidence, disciplined inquiry, and a commitment to explaining markets with intellectual clarity. AQR institutionalizes this identity through a public research platform that treats publication as part of the firm's purpose, not a marketing add-on (AQR Capital Management, n.d.-a; AQR Capital Management, n.d.-b; Mark and Pearson 2001).

Show Traits in Action: AQR lives the Sage through codified reasoning. Instead of relying on charisma or mystery, it publishes frameworks, white papers, and journal-style articles that articulate how it thinks about risk premia, diversification, and systematic investing. This creates a recognizable "AQR voice": analytical, explanatory, and intellectually accountable. The brand becomes legible because the firm repeatedly shows its work—ideas are presented, tested, debated, refined, and archived (AQR Capital Management, n.d.-b; AQR Capital Management, n.d.-c).

Conflict (Weakness): Every Sage carries a weakness: the risk of appearing too intellectual, too clinical, or too distant from lived market experience. When a firm's identity is strongly tied to published frameworks, it can be judged harshly when market regimes challenge those frameworks. Under stress, research-driven brands face a particular skepticism: "Is this wisdom—or rationalization?" The very transparency that builds credibility can amplify scrutiny because claims are explicit and preserved.

Resolution: AQR endures by doing what Sages do: returning to first principles and continuing to teach through uncertainty. The brand stays coherent because it remains anchored to process, updating research, clarifying assumptions, and defending the integrity of the intellectual system rather than chasing short-term narrative shifts. In effect, AQR converts debate into durability: the brand is not threatened by questions; it is strengthened by them, because disciplined explanation is the product.

Allocator's Perspective: Allocators interpret AQR as intellectually consistent and committee usable. Labeling it a Sage helps an allocator explain the firm's identity quickly: a manager that leads with research, publishes its worldview, and invites evaluation of reasoning rather than charisma. In a crowded field, that archetype becomes shorthand for what the allocator is buying: not only exposure, but a stable, documented philosophy that can be under-written across cycles.

In practice, we do not have enough time to tell long stories during a meeting or a conference call. Keeping them short, in simple story structures, works best.

For a story to truly stand out, it must possess the ability to attract attention, emotionally influence the audience, and transform their perspectives during the narrative. At the same time, many stories may have one or two of these attributes, but those that incorporate all three become memorable and impactful.

Where to Place the Story

Stories can be placed in any part of a presentation, meeting, or call. The choice is yours, as long as they are used sporadically and crafted well. You can use a story to "break the ice" at the very beginning, when explaining your investment process and how you came about discovering your alpha.

You can use a story when talking about the investment team or portfolio manager to portray their track record and investment style. Anecdotes related to the companies you have invested in can also be interesting to share, as well as stories about specific investment positions and how they evolved over time.

Keep the story short and effective, crafted and well placed.

Analysis:
Steven Schwarzman's Early Fundraising Story

Adapted from "What It Takes" (Schwarzman, 2019), Chapter 8: "Call, Then Keep Calling"

Steven Schwarzman's early fundraising story from *What It Takes* offers more than a glimpse into Blackstone's beginnings, it reveals a powerful narrative structure built on persistence, timing, and the psychology of the first "yes." Let's examine how his story un-folds and why it resonates so strongly with the audience.

Here is what he shared with us:

"To get us rolling we wrote to everyone we knew, more than 400 cheerful letters introducing our new firm. We wrote about our track records and reminisced about the business we had done together. We laid out our plans and asked for work. Then we sat back and waited. I was expecting the phone to ring nonstop. But on the few occasions it did ring, it was only to congratulate us and wish us luck. 'How about some business?' I would ask. 'Not right now, but we'll think about you in the future.'

The day after our advertisement appeared in the New York Times, I heard a knock at the door. I opened it to find a guy in leather pants, a black motorcycle jacket, and a little black leather motorcycle hat. We were waiting to hear from our familiar M&A clients, but we got the gang leader from the wild.

'Is there a Steve Schwarzman here?' he asked. 'What are you delivering?' I replied.

'I'm not delivering anything. My name is Sam Zell. Leah told me I should meet you.'

In 1979, we had hired Leah Zell at Lehman. She had been an English major at Harvard and had just earned her PhD. After talking with her for a few minutes, it was obvious she had an exceptional mind. Though she knew nothing about finance, I decided to give her a chance. Leah proved to be a terrific analyst. This biker was her brother.

'What's with the outfit?' I said.

'I left my motorcycle downstairs.' 'Where downstairs?' 'I chained it up on Park Avenue,' he said, to a hydrant.

Our first day. This is some future, I thought. He must have thought the same thing, looking at me sitting there in my suit in our bare office.

'Look, I'm sorry, we just moved in today. We've hardly got any furniture yet.'

'That's OK,' said Sam. He sat on the floor, leaned against the wall against our rolled-up rug, and began to talk. He owned real estate and wanted to buy some companies but didn't know much about finance.

'Why don't you teach me?' he said.

I later found out I shouldn't have been misled by the outfit. Sam's version of owning real estate meant he was building one of the largest portfolios of real estate in the country. All he told me that day was that he bought bankrupt properties and wanted to build an empire.

We spent two and a half hours sitting on the floor talking. In the years to come, we would do a lot of business together. This one unexpected visitor turned out to be worth more to Blackstone than all the clients we expected in those early days who never came."

Steven Schwarzman's story follows the classic narrative structure, a three-act arc of *Character, Conflict, and Resolution*, enriched by a *surprise-reversal* that makes it both memorable and instructive.

Act I: The story begins with the setup: Schwarzman, newly co-founding Blackstone, embodies the *Hero/Builder* archetype, ambitious, confident, and ready to conquer his first major challenge. He sends over four hundred letters to potential investors, expecting the phone to ring nonstop. This is the *Character* stage, where his intent and optimism set the emotional baseline.

Act II: Then comes the *Conflict.* Despite his credentials and enthusiasm, no one calls back. The silence becomes the obstacle, an invisible antagonist. This moment of rejection introduces tension and humility, humanizing Schwarzman and building empathy. The reader or listener feels the sting of unmet expectation, the deflation that often accompanies early-stage fundraising. It's the emotional dip that makes the story relatable and credible.

Act III: The *Resolution* arrives through a sharp reversal. Instead of the institutional investor Schwarzman hoped for, opportunity arrives in the form of Sam Zell, a man in leather pants and a motorcycle jacket. The unexpected visitor becomes the unexpected client. The moment is cinematic: a contrast between the world of Wall Street suits and a streetwise entrepreneur chained to his Har-ley on Park Avenue. The humor and irony create memorability, while the deeper meaning emerges, opportunity rarely looks the way we imagine it will.

This story works because it blends vulnerability, surprise, and transformation. It moves from expectation to disappointment, from frustration to astonishment, and finally to validation. The emotional rhythm keeps the listener engaged and the moral lands cleanly: stay open to the unexpected; your first investor may not look like the one you are waiting for.

From a branding perspective, the story positions Schwarzman and early Blackstone as pragmatic Heroes, resilient, opportunistic, and open to unconventional paths. It reveals the mindset of a builder who turns every encounter into potential. For allocators and founders alike, it is a timeless parable about humility, persistence, and the power of serendipity in the early stages of building something enduring.

Telling stories with data

Data is everything in the asset management industry. It is used to communicate investment insights, performance metrics, and market trends. When framed strategically, data becomes a powerful tool for engagement and differentiation. Hedge fund managers who master the art of data-driven storytelling not only elevate their brand but also enhance investor confidence.

The first step in using data to support a brand narrative starts with understanding the audience. Although institutional investors share similar investment acumen, they often differ in risk appetite and investment constraints. The messaging should be tailored to the specific profile of each institutional allocator.

Raw data, however accurate, does not speak for itself. We must find the story within the data, extracting meaningful insights, trends, anomalies, and inflection points that validate an investment philosophy. The most compelling data stories are those that directly address allocator priorities: repeatability of returns, robustness of process, risk mitigation, and portfolio fit. The narrative of the data, and the story surrounding it, must follow a logical flow and remain within the broader context of the strategy introduction.

Visual representation of data significantly improves understanding and retention of information. All visuals, charts, graphs, and tables, should be designed with clarity in mind: minimize clutter, avoid excessive granularity, and prioritize readability. The "less is more" principle works exceptionally well, enhancing comprehension and precision.

Data presented in isolation can be misleading or misinterpreted. We must provide sufficient context to help investors understand the significance of specific metrics. This includes interpreting performance within broader market conditions, explaining the rationale behind investment decisions, and showing how the data reflects the repeatability and discipline of the process. Context transforms statistics into meaning and fosters trust in the manager's approach.

CHAPTER SIX

Brand Implementation

The Brand Promoters:
Who Builds the Hedge Fund Brand?

A hedge fund's brand emerges from a broad ecosystem of internal and external stakeholders, rather than from any single function. Their collective actions, interactions, and decisions ultimately define how the firm is perceived.

Brand promotion extends far beyond marketing. Investment professionals, client-facing teams, operations, and external partners all influence how the firm is perceived. Their communications, behaviors, and execution must consistently reflect a unified brand narrative.

Internal Stakeholders: Direct Brand Custodians

Investment Leadership: Portfolio managers and CIOs are the most visible brand ambassadors. Their philosophy, commentary, and investor interactions anchor the firm's identity. Whether conferences, letters, or investor calls, their tone and messaging must align with the firm's strategic positioning. Senior investment leaders must internalize the brand platform—core message, allocator personas, and differentiators—to reinforce a consistent and credible value proposition. In many firms, the PM or CIO becomes synonymous with the brand itself.

Investor Relations: Investor Relations teams are the frontline stewards of the brand. Beyond relationship management, they translate performance, risk, process, and culture into a coherent allocator experience. Every touchpoint, pitchbooks, letters, DDQs, onboarding, shapes perception. Close alignment with investment and marketing teams is essential to avoid fragmented messaging and to maintain credibility and trust.

Operations and the COO: Operational excellence is an implicit brand promise. Reliability, precision, and scalability reinforce institutional confidence. Timely reporting, smooth onboarding, and responsive infrastructure all strengthen brand equity. Even behind-the-scenes communications, particularly during transitions, must reflect the firm's brand personality.

Legal and Compliance: Legal and compliance functions safe-guard both regulatory integrity and brand credibility. Their review of disclosures and public materials directly affects perception. During periods of scrutiny or crisis, these teams shape the firm's external posture. Preserving transparency and integrity while reinforcing brand values is critical.

Marketing and Communications: Marketing defines the brand narrative, visual identity, and messaging architecture. Its effectiveness depends on firm-wide adoption. A core responsibility is enablement: equipping investment, IR, and operations teams to express the brand consistently. Marketing should lead brand governance and serve as the central reference point for all communications.

External Stakeholders:
The Second Circle of Influence

Allocators and Clients: Institutional clients are powerful brand amplifiers. Peer references and informal endorsements shape allocator perception. Consistency between promise and experience is essential. Misalignment erodes trust; alignment converts clients into advocates.

Placement Agents and Advisors: Third-party marketers and consultants must be fully aligned with the firm's positioning and tone. Inconsistent language or messaging risks brand dilution. Standardized messaging frameworks and branding toolkits are essential for coherence across the fundraising ecosystem.

Vendors and Service Providers: Administrators, legal counsel, auditors, and compliance vendors contribute indirectly to brand perception. Their professionalism and reputation reinforce institutional credibility. Vendor selection should consider alignment with brand values, not just technical competence.

Media and Public Relations: Media and PR amplify the brand narrative. Without alignment, they can create reputational dissonance. Clear messaging guides, trained spokespersons, and disciplined media engagement are essential to maintaining brand integrity.

Unified Messaging and Brand Coherence

A hedge fund brand lives in every interaction—emails, meetings, reports, and data rooms. Brand equity is built or eroded through thousands of micro-moments.

Unified messaging and consistent tonality are foundational. Stakeholders must be trained and aligned to communicate with clarity and emotional consistency. Authenticity does not require uniformity, but it does require coherence.

The strongest hedge fund brands align culture, communication, and client experience. This alignment requires deliberate governance, internal training, external coordination, and continuous calibration.

When achieved, brand coherence becomes a durable competitive advantage.

Brand Guidance and Creative Standards

While messaging and visuals may evolve, the core identity must remain intact. A formal Brand Guidance Document preserves and scales that identity, ensuring alignment across teams, vendors, and partners.

A practical outline of such a guide is provided in the Appendix.

CHAPTER SEVEN

Brand Management

What is not reviewed eventually drifts.

Periodic Audit:
Institutional Brand Health as a Strategic Discipline

In the asset management industry, brands are not built once, they are stewarded over time. While investment performance fluctuates, brand perception must remain resilient, clear, and trusted. For this reason, periodic brand audits are essential, not as a marketing ritual but as a strategic discipline embedded within firm governance. Much like a risk review or compliance check, a brand audit is a mechanism for preserving relevance, reinforcing credibility, and aligning internal and external narratives.

A robust brand audit begins internally. Leadership must ask: do our portfolio managers, client-facing professionals, and marketing team share the same understanding of what our firm stands for? Is our investment philosophy communicated with clarity and consistency? Are we positioned around outdated value propositions, or are we articulating fresh relevance in a shifting industry landscape?

Externally, an audit must assess how the market truly perceives the brand. Are institutional allocators clear on our differentiators? Do consultants understand our edge beyond performance numbers? Does our website reflect our current capabilities, thought leadership, and ESG alignment, or is it a digital time capsule? The audit must also benchmark the firm's brand positioning against competitors, especially in saturated or commoditized segments where clarity is king.

The most effective audits culminate in a Brand Alignment Report, an actionable blueprint outlining what must be preserved, refined, or evolved. This may involve revisiting the firm's mission and origin story, tightening investment messaging, aligning visual identity with strategic priorities, or refreshing how intellectual capital is packaged and disseminated. For firms undergoing generational transition, entering new markets, or facing fundraising headwinds, the timing of an audit is even more critical.

Asset managers who treat their brand as a living asset, one that must be reviewed, measured, and refined, are far better positioned to endure market cycles, win mandates, and command mindshare with allocators.

Crisis Management:
When Brand Becomes the Last Line of Defense

Crises in the asset management industry do not send calendar invites. They arrive unannounced, through performance draw-downs, regulatory actions, reputational breaches, sudden departures, or geopolitical events that shake investor confidence. When such moments hit, brand becomes the last line of defense, the reservoir of trust that determines whether stakeholders give the firm room to recover or walk away.

It is about having built enough reputational equity beforehand that the market distinguishes a setback from systemic failure. A firm with a clearly defined, consistently communicated brand, one rooted in authenticity and values, has a far better chance of weathering storms. When allocators know what a firm stands for beyond numbers, they contextualize problems differently.

The anatomy of effective crisis brand management rests on three pillars. The first is internal alignment. Senior leadership must act swiftly and cohesively, aligning on the facts, the message, and the tone. Silence or internal discord is often more damaging than the crisis itself. The second is transparent, timely, and empathetic communication. Whether addressing clients, employees, media, or regulators, a clear narrative must be shared, acknowledging the issue, outlining the response, and reiterating the firm's commitment to its fiduciary duty and values.

The third pillar is stakeholder engagement. Direct outreach to key allocators, consultant gatekeepers, and trusted partners can preempt misinformation and signal accountability.

Consider the post-2008 landscape: firms that proactively communicated with investors during the liquidity crunch, not hiding behind PDFs but offering real-time updates and open dialogue, retained trust even when returns faltered.

Crisis does not destroy a strong brand; it reveals its strength. Firms that build reputational capital proactively through culture, consistent messaging, and values-driven leadership do not just survive crises, they define their legacy through them.

Adaptability:
Branding for a Market That Never Stands Still

Brand strength in asset management is not a fixed asset; it is a dynamic currency that must evolve in sync with a changing industry and shifting allocator expectations. As demographics, technology, and client behaviors reshape the competitive landscape, firms that thrive are those whose brands are not only authentic but also adaptable.

Today, adaptability is not optional. Passive products, fee compression, digital platforms, and generational wealth transfer are dismantling traditional distribution models. Institutional investors are increasingly ESG-conscious, data-driven, and skeptical of legacy claims. Meanwhile, the next wave of allocators, including Millennial CIOs, family office principals, and fintech platforms, consume information differently, engage digitally, and demand authenticity.

Adapting a brand does not mean abandoning its roots. It means translating core values into a modern voice. A 25-year-old boutique value manager, for example, may still deliver the same disciplined performance, but how is that story told today? Is it packaged in short-form video, shared in real-time thought leader-ship, and optimized for digital consumption? Or is it still buried in 20-page PDFs and decade-old conference slide decks?

Adaptability also involves tone and transparency. The old wall of institutional formality is giving way to a more human, story-driven approach. Firms that are willing to show their people, processes, and philosophy, not as jargon but as stories, build emotional resonance with allocators navigating complexity and choice overload.

Equally important is internal brand adaptability. Can the firm's professionals articulate its evolving story? Have they been trained to communicate in a way that is consistent across geographies, teams, and mediums? Are investor relations and portfolio management aligned in how they describe the strategy and its real-world impact?

Adaptability also means building feedback loops. The best brands listen. They measure allocator engagement, track digital analytics, ask for input, and respond to market shifts with agility. Brand success is no longer about being the loudest voice; it is about being the clearest and most relevant voice in a noisy and skeptical marketplace.

In the end, an adaptable brand is not one that chases trends. It is one that remains rooted in purpose while embracing new methods to express it. In a world where performance is unpredictable and products are commoditized, the firms that remain relevant are those whose brands evolve without losing their soul.

CHAPTER EIGHT

Examples of Effective Hedge Fund Branding

The case studies that follow examine hedge fund branding at the level that matters most: brand architecture in action. They show how identity is deliberately constructed, translated into a consistent voice and presence, and reinforced through the same repeatable signals, culture, communication discipline, proof artifacts, and institutional behavior, year after year. The objective is not to catalog transactions or headline campaigns, but to surface the brand patterns that drive recognition, credibility, and allocator confidence over a full market cycle.

Bridgewater Associates
Branding Through Intellectual Culture and Radical Transparency

Ray Dalio founded the firm in 1975, and the Bridgewater brand has long been associated with a distinctive cultural thesis: an "idea

meritocracy" pursued through "radical truth" and "radical transparency." Bridgewater's culture pages explicitly use this language and present it as an operating system rather than a marketing slogan.

From a branding perspective, Bridgewater demonstrates what "brand equals operating philosophy" looks like in practice. The firm's identity is not primarily visual; it is behavioral, ow decisions are argued, how truth is handled, and how norms are codified and trained. The Principles ecosystem reinforces this identity by publishing a structured framework describing an idea meritocracy built on radical transparency.

The brand also extends into tools. The "Dot Collector" was launched publicly as a real-time feedback tool designed to systematize micro-feedback, turning a cultural practice into a product. This is branding through instrumentation: the culture becomes tangible, teachable, and exportable.

Key branding elements

- Culture as identity: the operating system is the brand, idea meritocracy; radical transparency.
- Codified philosophy: values and behaviors are documented and taught via the Principles framework.

- Tools as brand proof: culture is reinforced by mechanisms, e.g., Dot Collector, rather than slogans.

Allocator takeaway: Allocators read this as process integrity: a firm whose behavior is disciplined, repeatable, and internally enforced. The culture-as-system signal reduces key-person ambiguity because the firm presents a structured decision framework, not just opinions It also raises a diligence question: Can we live with this level of internal candor and governance design?

Brand archetype: The Sage archetype. Bridgewater signals that knowledge, intellectual rigor, and structured reasoning are the central sources of authority in the organization. (Mark & Pearson, 2001).

Pershing Square Capital Management
Brand as Public Narrative Discipline

The Pershing Square brand is built around public argument, a manager that communicates in a way designed to be scrutinized. What matters here is not any single campaign, but the communications architecture: formal letters, presentations, and investor updates that keep the narrative coherent over time.

Pershing Square Holdings maintains a dedicated "Materials" hub organizing letters and presentations—signaling an intentional posture: investors should be able to see how the firm thinks, what it owns, and how it explains itself. This is branding through documentary consistency.

The signature is repeatability: publish the rationale, keep a tight narrative, and treat communication as a system rather than periodic marketing. The structure—memos, annual decks, archived investor materials—becomes a recognizable brand asset.

Key branding elements

- Narrative cadence: predictable rhythm of letters and presentations builds trust through consistency.
- Public "thinking style": the firm's voice is part of the product, explicit, argumentative, accountable.
- Library effect: a permanent archive turns communication into enduring brand equity.

Allocator takeaway: Allocators interpret this as accountability and transparency-by-design: you are giving them a durable record of decision-making, not just a quarterly performance explanation. It strengthens confidence in governance and clarity, but it also increases reputational sensitivity: public narrative discipline must remain high under stress because mistakes are visible and searchable.

Brand archetype: The Hero. Pershing Square brand is built on conviction, confrontation, and the willingness to be judged publicly, it steps into scrutiny rather than avoiding it. (Mark & Pearson, 2001).

Elliott Investment Management
Understated Power and Reputation-Led Branding

Elliott's brand is intentionally restrained. The firm positions itself as one of the oldest fund managers of its kind under continuous management, emphasizing endurance and institutional seriousness.

The brand is also structured around founder authority and continuity. Elliott's official biography page for Paul Singer states he founded the firm in 1977, reinforcing a lineage narrative: longevity, discipline, and control.

Branding-wise, Elliott illustrates how a firm can project dominance through selective visibility: minimal outward content, limited self-promotion, and an identity that travels via reputation and institutional memory rather than constant publishing. The scarcity is the signal.

Key branding elements

- Longevity as a pillar: "continuous management" creates durability credibility.
- Founder continuity cue: lineage and authority rooted in the origin story.
- Scarcity strategy: low public output can amplify exclusivity and control.

Allocator takeaway: Allocators interpret this as institutional power and discretion—a firm that prioritizes outcomes over publicity and does not need marketing volume to be taken seriously. The diligence trade-off is access and opacity: the allocator must be comfortable underwriting a manager where reputation substitutes for content, and where engagement may be selective.

Brand archetype: The Ruler. Elliott's brand is built around control, authority, and institutional command. It signals power through endurance, discipline, and selective engagement rather than visibility. (Mark & Pearson, 2001).

Five Branding Patterns Allocators Actually Reward

1. The operating system is the brand

Allocators reward firms whose "brand" is not a slogan but a repeatable way of making decisions, visible internal logic that can be analyzed; how truth is handled, how disagreement is resolved, how conviction is built. Bridgewater Associates is the clearest example: its public culture framing emphasizes "radical truth" and "radical transparency" as an operating model.

2. A persistent "proof library" beats performance storytelling

Allocators reward firms that build a durable archive of primary artifacts, letters, presentations, research, or formal reporting, so the firm can be evaluated on a long record of thinking, not a single pitch. Pershing Square Holdings maintains a centralized materials archive: letters, fact sheets, presentations.

3. Communication cadence signals governance

Allocators reward managers who communicate with predictable rhythm and structure, because cadence is a proxy for internal discipline, controls, and stakeholder respect. The regular letters, presentations, standardized updates, functions like a governance signal: the organization can explain itself consistently and with-stand scrutiny.

Allocator takeaway: a firm that can keep its narrative coherent in normal times is more likely to keep it coherent during drawdowns and controversy.

4. Selective visibility can increase perceived institutional quality

Allocators do not always reward loudness. They often reward constraint, a firm that communicates deliberately and does not over-market. Elliott Investment Management is a strong case of founder continuity and restrained outward posture; its own profile emphasizes founder identity and longevity.

5. Talent-market credibility is brand equity

Allocators reward brands that signal capability density, the ability to recruit and retain the exact talent the strategy requires and to keep a learning system alive. Across these examples, successful hedge fund brands share three core traits:

Authenticity: The brand aligns with the internal culture and investment philosophy of the firm. There is no disconnect between what is promised and what is practiced.

Clarity: Each brand communicates a clear, differentiated narrative, whether it is innovation, precision, or conviction.

Consistency: Branding is reinforced across every touchpoint, including founder communications, investor reports, recruiting, media, and performance positioning.

141

CHAPTER NINE

Brand as an Asset

Brand is the only asset that appreciates before it is measured.

Brand Equity:
The Intangible Engine Behind Asset Growth

In the world of asset management, where performance data and market cycles often dominate conversations, brand equity remains a quiet but formidable force, an asset in its own right. Brand equity refers to the perceived value a firm holds in the minds of clients, intermediaries, regulators, and employees.

Unlike portfolio returns, brand equity is intangible, cumulative, and resilient.

For asset managers, brand equity accrues through consistent alignment of messaging, mission, and market reputation over time. It encapsulates both functional trust (for example, the firm's ability to deliver alpha or manage risk prudently) and emotional trust (for example, integrity, vision, and long-term orientation) that clients place in the organization. This combination fosters brand loyalty, pricing power, investor patience, and the ability to weather market volatility without eroding the AUM.

For emerging managers, brand equity may begin with a founder's personal credibility, academic pedigree, prior track record, or unique insight into a niche strategy. But to scale, equity tend to shift from personal to organizational. This involves articulating a clear value proposition, reinforcing it through every touchpoint (from pitchbooks to press coverage), and living the brand through investor communication and firm culture.

An often-overlooked component of brand equity in asset management is continuity. Allocators are wary of "style drift" and interpret erratic brand behavior as a signal of internal uncertainty. Consistency over time, especially during downturns, reinforces trust. In fact, some of the most powerful branding moments occur not during bull markets but in how firms respond to stress. A brand that communicates clearly during drawdowns, stands by its process, and avoids knee-jerk repositioning strengthens its long-term equity.

Brand equity also impacts recruiting, retention, and partnerships. Top investment talent is attracted to firms with strong reputations and alignment with their personal values. Similarly, consultants, platforms, and OCIOs are more likely to include high-equity brands in their recommended lists. When a brand reaches a certain threshold of equity, it becomes self-reinforcing; each win amplifies the next.

In summary, brand equity is not simply an output of good performance; it is an asset that can be consciously designed, invested in, and compounded over time. In a sector where differentiation is difficult and commoditization looms large, brand equity offers the clearest path to long-term strategic advantage. It is the hidden balance sheet of the modern asset manager.

ROI on Branding: Quantifying the Intangible

In the accountability-driven realm of asset management, every dollar spent must ultimately justify its existence. This is especially true for branding investments, which are frequently seen as "soft costs" in a culture dominated by basis points and quantifiable alpha. Yet, when approached strategically, branding yields measurable returns, both direct and indirect, that can enhance enterprise value, fundraising capacity, and operational efficiency.

Understanding and demonstrating the return on investment (ROI) of branding is essential for positioning it not as a luxury, but as a necessity. The ROI on branding in asset management can be measured in several key dimensions: capital raising efficiency, margin expansion, client retention, talent acquisition, and strategic optionality. Each of these contributes to the firm's long-term enterprise value.

Capital Raising Efficiency

One of the most immediate and observable benefits of a strong brand is improved fundraising velocity. A clearly articulated brand reduces friction in the sales cycle by pre-positioning the firm in the allocator's mind before the first meeting. Brand-aware firms report shorter conversion times, higher meeting-to-investment ratios, and better receptivity in competitive mandates.

For instance, a well-crafted brand identity and consistent messaging have been shown to increase pitchbook-to-meeting conversions by up to 30% (Cerulli Associates, 2021). A study by Cerulli Associates also noted that brand reputation is among the top three factors influencing consultant recommendations, often ahead of recent performance.

Margin Expansion

Managers with strong brands are better positioned to defend fees. In an era of compression, particularly in passive and quasi-passive strategies, brand is one of the few levers available to preserve pricing integrity.

Firms like AQR, which consistently invest in thought leader-ship and transparent communication (AQR, 2022), have built reputations that allow them to command a premium over lower-cost replicators.

Client Retention and Lifetime Value

A compelling brand does not just attract capital, it retains it. Asset managers with strong brand trust often experience lower redemptions during periods of underperformance. This stickiness enhances the predictability of revenue and reduces the cost of reacquiring lost AUM. Retention is a function of brand equity, and its economic value is substantial.

According to Bain & Company (2023), increasing customer retention by just 5% can increase profits by 25% to 95%.

Additionally, client lifetime value increases as strong brands create room for cross-selling new products and expanding wallet share across mandates.

Talent and Organizational ROI

The ROI of branding extends beyond the external market into internal alignment and talent acquisition. Strong brands attract high-performing professionals who seek purpose, stability, and industry prestige. This reduces recruiting costs, accelerates cultural alignment, and contributes to organizational resilience.

In today's market, where young talent values purpose as much as pay, a brand that clearly articulates mission and values becomes a competitive advantage.

Strategic Optionality and Exit Value

Brand strength also confers strategic optionality. Well-branded asset managers are more attractive targets for partnerships, minority investments, and acquisitions. Their value is not limited to fee revenue; it includes goodwill, brand recognition, distribution relationships, and client trust. These elements command premium valuations.

Quantifying branding ROI requires a shift in mindset: from viewing branding as an expense to managing, it as a capital investment. This involves tracking not only hard metrics (e.g., AUM inflows, fee compression avoidance, lead conversrions), but also soft indicators (e.g., brand recall, sentiment analysis, media visibility).

Tools like Net Promoter Score (Reichheld, 2003), brand lift studies, and CRM attribution models (Forrester, 2021) can provide structured frameworks for assessing effectiveness.

Branding, when approached with the same discipline as portfolio management, becomes a force multiplier. It is the lever that turns visibility into credibility, and credibility into capital. In a market increasingly defined by transparency and competition, the ROI on branding is not only real; it may be the most underappreciated alpha source of all.

The Future of
Hedge Fund Branding

The hedge fund industry is entering an era where endurance, not exclusivity, defines success. Performance remains vital, but it no longer stands alone. Investors increasingly demand clarity of identity, alignment of values, and consistency of voice.

Branding in this future is less about ornament and more about architecture, the framework that signals resilience and purpose in a noisy, competitive marketplace. Funds that invest in building brands grounded in authenticity will create trust that persists long after quarterly returns have faded from memory.

Technology as a Branding Catalyst

Technology is becoming central to this shift. Artificial intelligence is already transforming how managers analyze markets, but its role in branding is just beginning. AI can personalize investor communications, analyze sentiment across allocator communities, and even generate insights that make a fund's thought leadership sharper and more relevant. At the same time, blockchain is reshaping transparency. Tokenized funds, immutable reporting systems, and blockchain-verified track records promise to change how investors assess credibility.

Branding will increasingly hinge on demonstrating not just performance, but also technological fluency and forward-looking innovation. A hedge fund's identity will, in part, be measured by how it integrates these tools to build trust and showcase accountability.

Governance, Culture, and Coherence

Equally important will be the integration of governance and culture into the brand itself. Investors are underwriting not only a strategy but also an institution. The strongest brands of the future will signal coherence: alignment between what is promised and what is delivered, between the values declared and the culture lived, between the story told and the results achieved.

Brand integrity demonstrated this way creates endurance. It reassures allocators that, regardless of market conditions, the fund knows who it is and will remain true to that identity, while also embracing the innovations that define the financial world of tomorrow.

Identity as a Competitive Advantage

The hedge fund world is more complex, transparent, and demanding than ever before. Numbers open the door, but identity keeps it open. Identity will increasingly be shaped by technology; AI will allow funds to communicate with precision and scale, while blockchain will provide investors with a new level of verifiable trust. Managers who weave these tools into their branding, not as gimmicks but as authentic extensions of their philosophy, will be positioned to thrive.

A Living Expression of Trust and Purpose

The future of hedge fund branding will belong to those who treat brand as a strategic asset rather than a decorative afterthought, a living expression of purpose, discipline, innovation, and trust. Managers who rise to this challenge will not only attract capital; they will earn durable partnerships that endure market cycles.

What the Storm Ultimately Revealed

That morning, in the first days of the pandemic, feels distant now. I still see the coffee cooling as the headlines rolled in, steady and unrelenting. Over time, it became clear what those moments set in motion.

The pandemic created opportunity, but it unfolded unevenly. After the losses of early 2020, hedge funds went on to compound positive returns through much of the following five years, yet a small group of managers captured a disproportionate share of investor capital. As one institutional allocator put it, *"We didn't back who moved fastest. We backed who we understood best when everything was breaking."*

In the end, the storm revealed a simple truth: branding is not about being seen; it is about being understood when it matters most.

152

Appendix

The concepts in this book are most powerful when translated into practice. To support that transition, the following frameworks are provided. They are designed to help hedge fund managers and asset leaders move from theory to action, asking sharper questions, clarifying identity, and aligning with the needs of investors.

Creating a strong brand for a hedge fund involves several key steps, each requiring introspection and strategic planning.

Brand Discovery

The brand discovery phase is crucial for laying the foundation of a hedge fund's brand identity. Here are more questions to consider during this phase.

1. Core Values and Mission:

- What are the fundamental beliefs that drive our organization?
- How do our values influence our investment decisions and client interactions?
- What is our mission statement, and how does it reflect our purpose?

2. Unique Value Proposition:

- What specific benefits do we offer that our competitors do not?
- How do our investment strategies set us apart in the market?

- What successes or case studies can we highlight to demonstrate our value?

3. Target Audience:

- What are the demographics and psychographics of our ideal investors?
- What are the primary concerns and goals of our target audience?
- How do our services align with the needs and expectations of our investors?

4. Market Positioning:

- What is the current perception of our brand in the market?
- How do we want to be perceived by our investors and peers?
- What gaps exist in the market that we can fill with our offerings?

5. Competitive Analysis:

- Who are our main competitors, and what are their strengths and weaknesses?
- How do we compare to them in terms of performance, reputation, and client satisfaction?

- What lessons can we learn from their branding strategies?

6. Internal Assessment:

- What are our key strengths and competitive advantages?
- What challenges or weaknesses do we need to address?
- How do our team's skills and expertise contribute to our brand identity?

7. Brand Personality:

- What adjectives best describe our brand's personality (e.g., innovative, trustworthy, dynamic)?
- How do we want our investors to feel when they interact with our brand?
- What stories or anecdotes can we share that embody our brand personality?

8. Vision for the Future:

- Where do we see our hedge fund in the next 5 to 10 years?
- How does our brand need to evolve to support our long-term goals?
- What role do we want to play in the broader financial industry?

Brand Strategy

The brand strategy phase involves defining how a hedge fund will communicate its identity and value proposition to its target audience. Here are more questions to consider during this phase.

1. Message Development

- What are the key messages we want to communicate to our audience?
- How can we simplify complex investment concepts to make them accessible to our investors?
- What stories or analogies can we use to illustrate our investment approach and successes?

2. Perception and Positioning

- How do we want to be perceived in the minds of our investors and the broader market?
- What positioning statement can we craft that clearly defines our place in the market?
- How can we leverage our strengths to enhance our market positioning?

3. Brand Attributes

- What specific attributes (e.g., innovation, reliability, transparency) do we want to be associated with our brand?
- How can we consistently convey these attributes across all touchpoints?
- What evidence or proof points can we provide to support these attributes?

4. Audience Engagement

- What are the most effective channels for reaching and engaging our target audience?
- How can we tailor our communication to different segments of our audience?
- What type of content will resonate most with our investors (e.g., reports, webinars, articles)?

5. Competitive Differentiation

- How can we clearly articulate what makes us different from our competitors?
- What unique benefits or experiences can we offer that others cannot?
- How can we capitalize on market trends to enhance our differentiation?
- What feedback mechanisms can we implement to continually improve the investor experience?

6. Crisis Management

- How will we handle potential challenges or crises that could impact our brand?
- What communication strategies can we put in place to maintain trust during difficult times?
- How can we proactively address investor concerns and manage expectations?

7. Long-Term Vision

- How does our brand strategy align with our long-term business objectives?
- What milestones or goals do we need to achieve to realize our brand vision?
- How will we measure the success of our brand strategy over time?

By addressing these questions, hedge funds can develop a robust brand strategy that effectively communicates their value, differentiates them from competitors, and fosters strong relationships with their investors.

Brand Identity

In the brand identity phase, hedge funds focus on developing the tangible and intangible elements that represent their brand. Here are more questions to consider during this phase.

1. Visual Identity

- What colors, fonts, and design elements best reflect our personality and values?
- How can our logo encapsulate our brand essence and be easily recognizable?
- Are there any visual symbols or icons that can reinforce our brand message?

2. Brand Voice and Tone

- What tone (e.g., formal, conversational, authoritative) should we use in our communications?
- How can we ensure our voice is consistent across different platforms and materials?
- How should our tone vary when addressing different audiences or contexts?

3. Brand Story

- What is the story behind our hedge fund's founding and evolution?
- How can we weave our brand story into our communications to create an emotional connection?
- What anecdotes or milestones can highlight our journey and achievements?

4. Cultural Alignment

- How does our brand identity align with our organizational culture and values?
- What internal practices or rituals can reinforce our brand identity among employees?
- How can we ensure that our team embodies our brand values in their interactions?

5. Emotional Appeal

- What emotions do we want to evoke in our investors when they engage with our brand?
- How can our brand identity create a sense of trust, security, and confidence?
- What elements of our identity can foster a personal connection with our audience?

6. Consistency and Flexibility

- How can we maintain consistency in our brand identity across all touchpoints?

- What guidelines or standards should we establish to ensure brand consistency?
- How can we remain flexible to adapt our identity to changing market conditions or trends?

7. Brand Touchpoints

- What are the key touchpoints where investors interact with our brand (e.g., website, reports, events)?
- How can we ensure that each touchpoint delivers a cohesive and positive brand experience?
- What improvements can we make to enhance the investor journey at each touchpoint?

8. Feedback and Iteration

- How will we gather feedback on our brand identity from investors and stakeholders?
- What criteria will we use to assess the effectiveness of our brand identity?
- How can we iterate and refine our identity based on feedback and evolving needs?

By exploring these questions, hedge funds can craft a compelling and authentic brand identity that resonates with their target audience and supports their strategic goals.

Brand Implementation

In the brand implementation phase, the focus is on executing the brand strategy and ensuring that the brand identity is consistently communicated across all platforms and interactions. Below are key questions to consider during this phase.

1. Communication Channels

- What are the most effective channels for reaching our target audience (e.g., digital, print, events)?
- How can we tailor our messaging to suit each channel while maintaining brand consistency?
- What is our strategy for integrating new communication technologies or platforms?

2. Team Training and Alignment

- How will we train our team to understand and embody our brand values and messaging?
- What tools or resources can we provide to help our team communicate our brand effectively?
- How can we encourage and measure brand advocacy among employees?

3. Content Creation

- What types of content (e.g., articles, videos, podcasts) will best engage our audience?
- How can we ensure that our content aligns with our brand identity and strategic goals?
- What is our process for content planning, creation, and distribution?

4. Brand Guidelines

- What specific guidelines will we establish to ensure brand consistency across all materials?
- How will we enforce these guidelines and address any deviations?
- How often will we review and update our brand guidelines?

5. Investor Experience

- How can we create a seamless and positive experience for investors at every touchpoint?
- What processes can we implement to gather and act on investor feedback?
- How can we personalize interactions to strengthen relationships with investors?

6. Monitoring and Measurement

- What metrics will we use to measure the success of our brand implementation?
- How will we track brand perception and engagement over time?
- What tools or platforms will assist us in monitoring our brand's performance?

7. Adaptation and Flexibility

- How will we adapt our brand implementation strategy to respond to market changes or feedback?
- What mechanisms do we have in place to quickly address any brand-related issues?
- How can we remain agile while maintaining brand consistency?

8. Partnerships and Collaborations

- What potential partnerships or collaborations can enhance our brand reach and credibility?
- How can we ensure that partners align with our brand values and identity?
- What criteria will we use to evaluate the success of these partnerships?

By addressing these questions, hedge funds can effectively implement their brand strategy, ensuring that their brand identity is consistently and authentically communicated to their target audience.

Brand Evaluation and Adaptation:

In the brand evaluation and adaptation phase, hedge funds focus on assessing the effectiveness of their brand strategy and making necessary adjustments to stay relevant and competitive. Below are key questions to guide this process.

1. Performance Assessment

- What key performance indicators (KPIs) are we using to evaluate our brand's success?
- How have our brand awareness and perception changed over time?
- What feedback have we received from investors, and how does it align with our brand goals?

2. Market and Competitive Analysis

- How have market trends or changes in the competitive landscape affected our brand?
- What are our competitors doing differently, and how might that impact our brand strategy?
- Are there new opportunities or threats in the market that we need to address?

3. Audience Insights

- How have the needs and preferences of our target audience evolved?
- Are there new segments of potential investors we should consider targeting?
- What insights can we gather from investor interactions to refine our brand approach?

4. Brand Consistency

- Are we maintaining consistency in our brand messaging and identity across all platforms?
- What areas of our brand implementation have deviated from our guidelines, and why?
- How can we ensure that all team members are aligned with our brand standards?

5. Adaptation Strategies

- What aspects of our brand strategy need to be adapted to better meet our objectives?
- How can we innovate or refresh our brand to remain relevant and engaging?
- What new technologies or platforms can we leverage to enhance our brand presence?

6. Internal Alignment

- How well is our team embodying and communicating our brand values?
- What additional training or resources might be needed to strengthen internal brand alignment?
- How can we foster a culture of continuous improvement in brand communication?

7. Long-Term Vision

- How does our current brand strategy align with our long-term business goals?
- What milestones have we achieved, and what future goals should we set?
- How can we ensure that our brand evolves alongside our business growth?

8. Feedback and Iteration

- What mechanisms do we have in place to gather ongoing feedback from stakeholders?
- How often will we review and update our brand strategy and guidelines?
- How can we create a process for iterative improvements based on real-time insights?

By exploring these questions, hedge funds can effectively evaluate their brand's performance and make informed adaptations to ensure continued success and relevance in the market. These questions serve as practical guidance for developing a comprehensive and effective brand strategy that resonates with target audiences and supports long-term business objectives.

Understanding allocator personas is critical for hedge fund leaders seeking to build brands that resonate with institutional investors. This guide provides detailed breakdowns of key allocator archetypes, along with branding implications and insights to tailor your approach.

Family Office Principal

Investment Motivations

Family Office Principals seek capital preservation with moderate growth. They are drawn to alternative investments to diversify beyond traditional markets and are often driven by multi-generational wealth goals and legacy considerations.

What They Are Solving For

- Preserving purchasing power in inflationary environments.
- Accessing managers with aligned values and personalized attention.
- Finding unique, off-market opportunities unavailable to larger institutions.

Communication Tone That Resonates

- Relationship-first, emphasizing trustworthiness and long-term partnership.
- Use storytelling to humanize the investment approach.
- Highlight alignment of interests, such as GP commitment and co-investments.

What Raises Red Flags

- Overly complex jargon without practical context.
- Lack of transparency around fees or strategy risks.
- Perceived arrogance or unwillingness to provide direct principal access.

Endowment Chief Investment Officer (CIO)

Investment Motivations

Endowment CIOs seek long-term returns to support spending needs and perpetuity goals. They focus on total portfolio construction and risk-adjusted returns.

What They Are Solving For

- Balancing liquidity for annual payouts with exposure to less liquid alternatives.
- Identifying alpha-generative managers to complement internal capabilities.
- Managing reputational risks from external manager selection.

Communication Tone That Resonates

- Institutional rigor, demonstrating process discipline and robust governance.
- Data-driven narratives backed by clear, concise metrics.
- Emphasize operational excellence, including reporting standards and compliance culture.

What Raises Red Flags

- Lack of an articulated investment process or risk framework.
- Inconsistency between verbal narrative and written materials.
- Failure to address ESG considerations if institutionally relevant.

RIA Investment Committee

Investment Motivations

RIA investment committees seek to provide best-in-class solutions for high-net-worth clients. They are focused on downside protection and transparent fee structures.

What They Are Solving For

- Differentiating their offering in a crowded market.
- Outsourcing alternative allocations without compromising fiduciary duty.
- Communicating complex strategies simply to advisors and clients.

Communication Tone That Resonates

- Educational and approachable, simplifying complexity without diluting substance.
- Provide turnkey materials for committee approval and client conversations.
- Highlight scalability and compliance with RIA platforms.

What Raises Red Flags

- Heavy reliance on illiquid positions for client bases requiring quarterly liquidity.
- Perceived conflicts of interest, such as retrocessions or opaque fees.
- Sales-focused pitches that seem product-oriented rather than solution-driven.

Fund of Funds Analyst

Investment Motivations

Analysts at funds of funds are tasked with sourcing emerging and niche managers to complement core allocations. They prioritize due diligence and quantitative analysis.

What They Are Solving For

- Curating diversified portfolios across styles and geographies.
- Building relationships with next-generation managers ahead of institutional flows.
- Managing liquidity needs for their own investor base.

Communication Tone That Resonates

- Analytical and precise, focusing on process repeatability and performance drivers.
- Provide comprehensive data room materials, including DDQs and holdings transparency.
- Engage in iterative discussions with analyst teams to build credibility.

What Raises Red Flags

- Inconsistent performance attribution or over-reliance on a single "star" PM.
- Resistance to transparency on positions or risk metrics.
- Defensive responses during diligence processes.

Pension Fund Gatekeeper

Investment Motivations

Pension fund gatekeepers prioritize scale, stability, and governance in manager relationships. They are focused on liability matching and portfolio diversification.

What They Are Solving For

- Meeting actuarial targets within strict risk budgets.
- Ensuring external managers have institutional-grade infrastructure.
- Balancing low fees with access to high-conviction ideas.

Communication Tone That Resonates

- Authoritative yet humble, showing readiness for board-level scrutiny.
- Highlight operational platform, compliance culture, and risk oversight.
- Provide peer examples of success with similar allocators.

What Raises Red Flags

- Lack of scalability for large ticket sizes.
- Weak compliance, operational, or cybersecurity processes.
- Overemphasis on "personality-driven" strategies without succession planning.

Effective positioning is the foundation of every successful hedge fund brand; it shapes how a manager is perceived, understood, and ultimately selected. It determines how a manager is understood, remembered, and selected—not only at introduction, but across market cycles.

I. Strategy-Driven Positioning

1. **Clarify the Core Edge** – Define the true driver of alpha with precision, separating skill from market beta, leverage, timing, or favorable conditions.

2. **Define the Portfolio Role** – State exactly how the strategy functions within a portfolio and what problem it is designed to solve.

3. **Map the Competitive Landscape** – Identify strategic whitespace rather than benchmarking against direct peers.

4. **Narrate Strategy Evolution** – Show how the strategy has matured through research, testing, and experience, signaling learning rather than reinvention.

5. **Translate Complexity** – Replace technical language with clear, structured explanations that preserve substance while improving comprehension.

II.   Founder & Firm Positioning

6.   **Anchor in Founder DNA** – Link personal conviction, experience, and worldview directly to the investment philosophy without relying on personality alone.

7.   **Leverage Institutional Pedigree** – Frame prior experience as a source of discipline, process, and judgment rather than résumé signaling.

8.   **Define Investment Ethos** – Express values as decision-making filters that guide behavior under uncertainty.

9.   **Create a Signature Framework** – Name and structure what makes the process repeatable, governable, and defensible.

10. **Highlight Cultural Differentiation** – Show how culture shapes decision quality, collaboration, and risk behavior over time.

III.   Allocator-Centric Positioning

11. **Solve a Portfolio Problem** – Lead with the need the strategy addresses rather than the product itself.

12. **Speak Allocator Language** – Use metrics and concepts relevant to portfolio construction, risk management, and capital efficiency.

13. **Use Transparency Strategically** – Offer visibility where it reinforces trust and clarity without creating noise or distraction.

14. **Position for Longevity** – Emphasize governance, succession planning, and operational continuity.

15. **Build Thought Leadership** – Demonstrate independent thinking through consistent, disciplined insights rather than reactive commentary.

IV.   Narrative & Expression

16. **Craft a Clear Narrative** – Define a coherent "why now" that aligns strategy, context, and purpose.

17. **Use Archetypal Framing** – Add emotional clarity and memorability without sacrificing sophistication.

18. **Own a Belief System** – Anchor positioning in enduring principles that extend beyond market cycles.

19. **Visualize Identity** – Ensure design, structure, and aesthetics reflect investment philosophy and tone.

20. **Enforce Consistency** – Reinforce the same message across all touchpoints until it becomes synonymous with the firm.

V.   Market & Structural Tactics

21. **Target Precisely** – Focus on the most relevant capital sources rather than maximizing exposure.

22. **Leverage Partnerships** – Align with platforms, advisors, or institutions that reinforce credibility and positioning.

23. **Time the Narrative** – Align messaging with market conditions, allocator priorities, and structural shifts.

24. **Highlight Asymmetry** – Show how the strategy behaves differently in periods of stress or dislocation.
25. **Demonstrate Crisis Behavior** – Use real examples to illustrate discipline, communication, and decision-making under pressure.

VI.   Psychological & Communication Tactics

26. **Reframe Risk** – Present uncertainty as something managed through process, not avoided or obscured.

27. **Build Familiarity** – Allow repetition and consistency to compound trust over time.

28. **Lead with Story** – Use narrative to create context and meaning, then reinforce with data.

29. **Create Memorability** – Prioritize clarity and recall over volume and detail.

Show Strength with Self-Awareness – Acknowledge limitations and lessons learned as signals of maturity and credibility.

183

This Appendix outlines the core components of a comprehensive Brand Guidance Document. It serves as a reference for managers and third parties to ensure consistency across all external representations of the firm.

2. Brand Strategy Overview

Defines the firm's strategic foundation, including:

- Mission statement
- Long-term vision
- Investment philosophy
- Market positioning and differentiation

3. Brand Personality and Core Values

Articulates the firm's tone, character, and behavioral standards, including:

- Brand personality attributes
- Core values and how they are expressed in practice

4. Audience Personas and Messaging Frameworks

Establishes clarity around investor communication by defining:

- Key investor and stakeholder audiences
- Primary needs and concerns by audience type
- Core message pillars with approved sample language

5. Visual Identity System

Codifies visual standards to ensure consistency, including:

- Logo usage guidelines
- Color palette and typography
- Graphic and data-visualization styles
- Photography direction
- Approved presentation and document templates

6. Voice and Language Standards

Provides guidance on written and verbal communication, including:

- Tone of voice
- Style and grammar conventions
- Approved language and terms to avoid

7. Digital and Media Guidelines

Outlines standards for external visibility, including:

- Website structure and tone
- Social media and media interaction protocols (if applicable)
- Press and communications templates
- Compliance review considerations

8. Use Cases and Governance

Clarifies practical application through:

- Intended use of the guidance
- Content approval and escalation workflows
- Access to brand assets and shared repositories

Purpose of This Appendix

Clear brand guidance reduces inconsistency, protects reputation, and reinforces institutional discipline. When applied across all touchpoints, it ensures the firm presents a coherent, credible, and professional identity to allocators and stakeholders.

187

References

Adler, Alfred. 1989. Understanding Human Nature. Oneworld Publications.

Agarwal, Vikas, Narayan Y. Naik, and Jun Wang. 2021. "Crisis, Risk Management, and Hedge Fund Performance." Journal of Finance and Investment Analysis 10 (2): 45–67.

AIMA. 2008. AIMA's Roadmap to Hedge Funds (Appendix 1: The Origins of Hedge Funds). AIMA.

AQR Capital Management. 2022. Communicating Factor-Based Strategies with Institutional Clients. AQR Capital Management.

ARK Investment Management LLC. 2024. Big Ideas 2024: Disrupting the Norm, Defining the Future. Annual research report (PDF). https://assets.arkinvest.com/media/epjffmus/big-ideas-2024.pdf.

ARK Investment Management LLC. n.d. ARK Research White Papers. Accessed January 28, 2026. https://www.ark-invest.com/ white-papers.

Bain & Company. 2023. The Value of Customer Retention. Bain & Company.

Berger, Jonah. 2016. Invisible Influence: The Hidden Forces That Shape Behavior. Simon & Schuster.

Bet-David, Patrick, and Greg Dinkin. 2023. Choose Your Enemies Wisely: Business Planning for the Audacious Few. Portfolio / Penguin.

BlackRock. 2022. Branding and Distribution in Sustainable Investing. BlackRock.

Bollinger, François, Pablo Guidotti, and Florent Pochon. 2010. "A New Take on Commodity Branding and Storytelling." Capital Market Perspectives.

Bridgewater Associates. 2025. Company Overview. Bridgewater Associates.

Bridgewater Associates. n.d. Home. Accessed January 28, 2026. https://www.bridgewater.com/.

Cassidy, John. 2011. "Mastering the Machine." The New Yorker, July 25, 2011. https://www.newyorker.com/magazine/2011/07/25/mastering-the-machine.

Choo, Christine, and Colin Rathbone. 2019. "Influencer Marketing and Institutional Trust." Journal of Financial Communications 12 (1): 45–62.

Cialdini, Robert. 2006. Influence: The Psychology of Persuasion. Harper Business.

CIM (Center for Institutional Money). 2022. Institutional Allocation Trends Survey. CIM.

CIPD. 2020. Employer Branding: A Guide for HR Leaders. Chartered Institute of Personnel and Development.

Cleverley, W. O. 2020. "Brand Reputation and Asset Management." Journal of Corporate Branding 18 (3): 1–19.

Dalio, Ray. 2017. Principles: Life and Work. Simon & Schuster.

Dalio, Ray. 2022. Principles for Dealing with the Changing World Order. Avid Reader Press.

Deloitte. 2023. Global Investment Management Outlook. Deloitte.

eVestment. 2021. Institutional Investor Due Diligence Trends Re-port. eVestment.

Forrester Research. 2024. Brand Experience Index. Forrester Re-search.

Gallo, Carmine. 2018. Talk Like TED: The 9 Public-Speaking Secrets of the World's Top Minds. St. Martin's Press.

GlobeNewswire. 2023. "Global alternative assets remain resilient in 2023 amid economic uncertainty — Preqin Global Re-ports 2024." December 13, 2023. https://www.globenewswire. com/news-release/2023/12/13/2795289/0/en/Global-alterna-tive-assets-remain-resilient-in-2023-amid-economic-uncer-tainty-Preqin-Global-Reports-2024.html.

Greenwich Associates. 2021. Institutional Investor Research Study on Manager Selection. Greenwich Associates.

Hinge Research Institute. 2022. Inside the Buyer's Brain, Fourth Edition: Executive Summary. Hinge Marketing. Accessed January 28, 2026. https://hingemarketing.com/library/article/ inside-the-buyers-brain-fourth-edition-executive-summary.

HBR (Harvard Business Review). 2021. "How to Build Trust in Financial Services." Harvard Business Review.

Institutional Investor. 2024. "Renaissance's 2024 Rebirth." November 14, 2024. https://www.institutionalinvestor.com/ article/2dvuqcy4qmtotptwls0cg/corner-office/renaissanc-es-2024-rebirth.

Investopedia. 2022. "Who Is Ray Dalio?" Accessed January 28, 2026. https://www.investopedia.com/who-is-ray-dalio-4767973.

Keller, Kevin Lane. 2013. Strategic Brand Management. 4th ed. Pearson.

Kahneman, Daniel. 2011. Thinking, Fast and Slow. Farrar, Straus and Giroux.

Kotler, Philip, and Kevin Keller. 2016. Marketing Management. 15th ed. Pearson.

Maslow, A. H. 1943. "A Theory of Human Motivation." Psychological Review 50 (4): 370–396.

Mark, Margaret, and Carol S. Pearson. 2001. The Hero and the Outlaw: Building Extraordinary Brands Through the Power of Archetypes. McGraw-Hill.

McKinsey & Company. 2019. "Five Ways ESG Creates Value." McKinsey Quarterly.

Morgan, John. 2019. Brand Narrative and Investor Trust. Oxford University Press.

Morningstar. 2022. Fund Flows and Manager Selection Trends. Morningstar.

Pedersen, Lasse Heje. 2015. Efficiently Inefficient: How Smart Money Invests and Market Prices Are Determined. Princeton University Press.

Preqin. 2023. Service Providers in Alternatives 2023: Preqin Report (PDF). https://www.gsequity.com/preqin-2023-report. pdf.

Pyrford Financial Planning. 2024. "Renaissance Technologies: The greatest hedge fund of all? (updated for 2024)." Accessed January 28, 2026. https://www.pyrfordfp.co.uk/renaissance-technologies-the-greatest-hedge-fund-of-all/.

Quantified Strategies. 2025. "Jim Simons: Medallion Fund Returns and Performance." Accessed January 28, 2026. https://www. quantifiedstrategies.com/jim-simons-medallion-fund-re-turn/.

S&P Dow Jones Indices. 2020. S&P Risk Parity Indices Methodology (PDF). https://www.spglobal.com/spdji/en/documents/ methodologies/methodology-sp-risk-parity-indices.pdf.

SoFi. 2022. Investment Strategy Outlook. SoFi.

VIA Institute on Character. 2023. Character Strengths Survey. VIA Institute.

Vincent, R. 2002. "Archetypes and Branding Psychology." Hunting the Muse.

Wengrow, David. 2008. "Prehistories of Commodity Branding." Current Anthropology 49 (1): 7–34.

Wheeler, Alina, and Rob Meyar. 2016. Designing Brand Identity: An Essential Guide. Wiley.

Wikipedia. 2024. Bridgewater Associates. Wikipedia. Accessed January 28, 2026. https://en.wikipedia.org/wiki/Bridgewa-ter_Associates.

Wikipedia. 2024. Renaissance Technologies. Wikipedia. Accessed January 28, 2026. https://en.wikipedia.org/wiki/Renaissance_ Technologies.

Young, Liz. 2022. Investment Strategy Outlook. SoFi.

About the Author

Natasha B. Koprivica began her career on the trading floor of Fidelity Capital Markets, where she built a rigorous foundation in institutional trading and the mechanics of global financial markets.

She later became a founding executive and Senior Vice President at Venus Capital Management, an emerging market hedge fund. Over sixteen years, she helped scale Venus from a boutique start-up into a globally recognized authority on emerging markets, launching multiple funds, institutionalizing operations, and cultivating allocator relationships across pensions, endowments, and family offices.

In 2015, she founded Fibonacci Capital Advisors LLC, a boutique advisory platform dedicated to helping hedge fund founders, ETF issuers, and private managers sharpen their brands, institutionalize their operations, and raise capital worldwide. In this capacity, she has advised asset managers on several continents and partnered with some of the world's largest financial institutions on institutional distribution, growth strategy, and capital formation.

She is frequently called to serve on boards of start-up funds and private businesses for her insights into investor psychology, market entry, and business development strategy.

Natasha earned a BBA degree in Entrepreneurship and Finance from the Institut Franco-Américain de Management in Paris, France, and holds an MBA from the F.W. Olin Graduate School of Business at Babson College, with a concentration in entrepreneurship and finance. She also has an academic background in lasers and nuclear physics, as well as formal studies in the theory of music and composition.

Her work, and this book, reflect a guiding principle honed over more than two decades in global asset management: performance may open the door, but it is brand clarity and narrative integrity that sustain trust, inspire loyalty, and secure enduring mandates.

Acknowledgments

This book has been shaped by years of conversation with professionals who work where markets, judgment, and trust intersect. I am grateful to the allocators, investment committee members, and due diligence professionals who shared how decisions are made under pressure, and to the portfolio managers and founders who spoke openly about building firms across cycles. Their willingness to reflect candidly helped give this work its depth.

I am equally thankful to the marketing and business development leaders within asset management who challenged assumptions around communication and positioning, as well as to the research analysts and industry observers whose data and perspective grounded these ideas in evidence. Their questions, more than their answers, pushed this book toward greater clarity.

Finally, I am grateful for the encouragement of my friends and my family that carried this work forward and quietly affirmed that what lasts is rarely built in haste.

Investment & Legal Disclosure

This publication is provided for educational and informational purposes only and does not constitute, and should not be construed as, investment advice, a recommendation, or an offer or solicitation to buy or sell any securities, financial instruments, investment products, or investment strategies.

Nothing contained herein is intended to create, nor should be construed as creating, an investment advisory, fiduciary, or client relationship between the author, the publisher, and any reader. The information presented is not intended to be, and should not be relied upon as, legal, tax, accounting, or investment advice. Readers should consult their own independent professional advisors regarding the appropriateness of any investment, strategy, or transaction discussed.

Any references to specific securities, issuers, investment strategies, case studies, or market participants are illustrative only and do not constitute an endorsement, recommendation, or opinion regarding suitability or performance.

Past performance, hypothetical examples, and illustrative scenarios are not indicative of future results. All investments involve risk, including the possible loss of principal. There can be no assurance that any investment strategy, framework, or approach discussed will achieve its stated objectives or result in profits.

The views expressed are those of the author as of the date of publication and are subject to change without notice. The author and publisher make no representations or warranties, express or implied, regarding the accuracy or completeness of the information contained herein and expressly disclaim any liability arising from its use.